Best Wishes

Super Bowl Victory

When we completed that pass, I knew we were going to win the Super Bowl. I wasn't thinking about the championship ring or anything like that. I just had a feeling of great accomplishment. I was thinking personally then, instead of about the team. I thought to myself that there are only five or six other quarterbacks who have ever won the Super Bowl and now I was one of them. Usually I think about everything on a team basis, but right then I was thinking about myself. I felt a great deal of pressure leave me when I realized we were going to win.

I walked off the field with a feeling of satisfaction and accomplishment. The dressing room was really a madhouse. Everybody was pouring champagne on each other. I felt very happy for some of our players who probably never expected to play in the Super Bowl—guys like Carl Garrett, who was a castoff from another team, John Matuszak, who got cut by several other teams, and Dave Rowe, a journeyman who had been around a long time without getting a chance to play in the Super Bowl. Willie Hall was cut before the season started and here he was back with us in the Super Bowl. I was also happy for Coach John Madden and Al Davis. They dedicated their lives to winning the Super Bowl.

It was an emotional scene. I didn't cry but I almost did. I was just kind of gliding along with the whole thing. It's something when you see 250-pound men hugging each other around the neck with tears in their eyes. Big, tough men telling each other how much they love each other, and crying.

Being a part of that is really something—but the best part for me was standing back and watching it. I just watched them pour champagne and celebrate. It was certainly a day to remember . . .

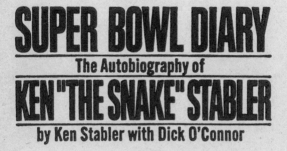

SUPER BOWL DIARY

The Autobiography of

KEN "THE SNAKE" STABLER

by Ken Stabler with Dick O'Connor

An Associated Features Book

PINNACLE BOOKS LOS ANGELES

SUPER BOWL DIARY: THE AUTOBIOGRAPHY OF KEN "THE SNAKE" STABLER

An original Pinnacle Books editon, published for the first time anywhere.

ISBN: 0-523-40-123-X

First printing, September 1977

Cover photos by Mickey Palmer/Focus on Sports

Printed in the United States of America

PINNACLE BOOKS, INC.
One Century Plaza
2029 Century Park East
Los Angeles, California 90067

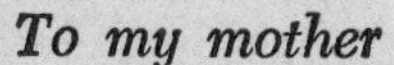

To my mother

ACKNOWLEDGMENTS

The making of this book wasn't a two-man job. For their help we wish to thank Al LoCasale and Andy Olsen of the Raiders, Tom LaMarre of the *Oakland Tribune*, Henry Pitts of Selma, Alabama, Joyce O'Connor, and the offensive line of the Oakland Raiders.

Ken Stabler and Dick O'Connor

Contents

Foreword

If you were to pick out the one quality that makes Ken Stabler the best quarterback in pro football, it's his leadership. When he says something, his teammates listen. When he tells them he's calling a play that will score a touchdown, it usually does.

When he told me not to worry during the Super Bowl, I didn't worry. He said we would score a lot of points and we did.

The success of the Oakland Raiders and my success as a coach have followed just about the same development as that of Ken Stabler. I was an assistant coach when he first came to the Raiders as a rookie in 1968. He had a knee operation and never played in a game. But there were some things you could tell from just talking to him. He had determination but I didn't see any signs of greatness in him because I didn't think he had a strong arm.

When he came back the next season, 1969, I was the head coach. That's when I realized that he had a talent that you can't teach—the ability to lead. It didn't make any difference what the situation was. Whenever we put him in the game, he moved the team. He did it the very first game he ever played, against the Dallas Cowboy rookies.

He wasn't really a good passer then but he moved the team. He didn't throw those darts like he does now and he knew he had to improve his arm. He spent a lot of time working with weights to strengthen his arm, because he didn't have much else to do. He was the third-string quarterback behind Daryle Lamonica and George Blanda.

In those days, he didn't even hold the ball for the extra points. That was very frustrating for him because I knew he thought he was good enough to be the starting quarterback on other teams in the league. He took out his frustration by building up his arms and shoulders. He got so he could really zip the ball.

When he was pissed off about not playing, he didn't sulk. He did something about it. He worked hard in practice to show us what he could do. Some guys are content to be a backup quarterback but Stabler wasn't. He made himself into a great player. But that didn't make him the starter because we had Lamonica and he was very good.

Stabler came in to me one day in 1973 and talked about his future with the Raiders and he wanted to know if he would ever get a chance to be the starter. I told him that talk didn't do any good. He had to show us he was the best quarterback. Well, we were going to play a game against St. Louis and he went out and ran the Cardinal plays against our defense. He was really great, so after that practice I told him he was going to be the starter.

He had a great game, we beat the Cardinals, and he's been the starter ever since.

Ken had the qualities of other great quarterbacks, a strong arm and confidence. But he has something else that makes him better than the others. It's his ability to store knowledge. There are lots of quarterbacks you can tell to do something and they'll go right out and do it. But with Stabler you tell him to do something in a certain situation. It might be when he gets a particular defense against us or at a specific point on the field.

Stabler remembers and, when the times comes, he does it. It might be an hour and a half later. Hell, it might be the next week. But when the situation we talked about comes up, he'll call the play I told him to.

That's what makes a winning quarterback.

There are a lot of football players who are smart. Some of them have knowledge but they can't use it. Others have lots of ideas but they are not smart enough to use them at the right time. To me, being a smart quarterback is having the knowledge and knowing when to use it. That's what the hell the game of football is all about.

Confidence? He exudes it. When he calls a play in the huddle, everyone knows it's going to work. Stabler has this air about him that makes others believe in what he says. His attitude is amazing. He never gets excited. He's the same when I'm talking to him during a Wednesday afternoon practice as he is when we are behind by three points with a minute to play on Sunday.

The one thing I'll never forget is that moment in the Super Bowl after we missed a field goal and then messed up another chance to score. I was really mad and was jumping up and down on the sidelines. Stabler came out of the game, came over and grabbed my arm.

He told me not to worry, that we would score lots of points and win the Super Bowl.

I felt like a little kid who was crying and someone gave me a sucker.

John Madden
Head Coach
Oakland Raiders

SUPER BOWL DIARY:
THE AUTOBIOGRAPHY OF
KEN "THE SNAKE" STABLER

1

Super Bowl

From the beginning Alabama quarterbacks were bound for glory in the Super Bowl. First Bart Starr guided Vince Lombardi's Packers to two lopsided victories. Then Joe Namath put his arm where his mouth was and the Jets shocked the Colts—and the haughty National Football League.

The tide turned away from Tuscaloosa for awhile, and quarterbacks from Purdue, Michigan State, Navy, and Louisiana Tech dominated Super Sunday headlines. But there was another star from Alabama waiting in the wings. And waiting. And waiting. Ken Stabler must have felt he was star-crossed; he and the Raiders had come close so often.

Then in 1976 they breezed through the season with only one defeat and earned a trip to Super Bowl XI in Pasadena, California. Their op-

ponents would be the Vikings, another team with a can't-win-the-big-ones label. After defeating the world champion Steelers, 24–7, for the American Football Conference title, the Raiders took a week off before opening their training camp at the seaside resort of Newport Beach, about 50 miles from the Rose Bowl, where Super Bowl XI would be played on January 9, 1977.

We wanted Super Bowl week to be as much like a week during the regular season as we could make it. Coach Madden kept telling us it would be just another game but we knew it wouldn't be and so did he.

There's a league rule that the teams have to be at their training site for the Super Bowl a week before the game. We went to Newport Beach on Monday—exactly a week before the game.

The first thing you do in a situation like this is to get familiar with the surroundings. Pete Banaszak, Fred Biletnikoff and I like to hang around together and we got rooms near each other. We're running buddies. We wanted to make sure we would have a car so we could hit the bars when we had the time. The hotel where we stayed—the Marriott—was nice. They had meeting rooms for us and it was in a good location. We had to take a bus to our practice field at University of California at Irvine, but it wasn't far.

We had our first practice on Tuesday. It was just like a Tuesday workout during the regular season, very light. Just enough to get us loosened up. The rest of the week was normal too. Wednesday was offense day, Thursday was defense, and Friday special teams. Then on Saturday we had a short review of everything we had worked on during the week. The workouts went well. There was no pressure. It was a good week.

On Saturday night we moved to the Beverly Hilton Hotel because Coach Madden didn't want it to be a long drive the morning of the game. Newport Beach is about 90 minutes from the Rose Bowl and the Hilton is only about 20.

I just relaxed the night before the game. I had a couple of drinks in my room. Biletnikoff and Banaszak came over and we just shot the bull. I always carry a bottle of scotch with me because it helps me relax.

I bought all the newspapers to see what the media was saying. You're always interested in what other people think about the game. Some were still saying the same thing about us not being able to win the big game. But hell, Minnesota never won any big games either.

I just stayed there in the room and watched TV. My lawyer, Henry Pitts, came by and we talked. Nothing special, just football talk.

The lobby of the hotel was a madhouse because some of the Oakland Raider boosters were staying there. We didn't even go down. If we wanted candy or magazines, we sent down for them. I just sipped my scotch and watched TV. I'm a night person and don't go to sleep early. I can't go to sleep at 10 or 11 o'clock. I finally went to sleep about 1:30 or 2 in the morning. I slept like a rock.

They woke us up for an 8 o'clock team breakfast. I wasn't excited, really. I had the usual steak and eggs. That's what they give everybody unless you want something different.

Then we had a short team meeting. John Madden gave us a little pep talk but he really didn't say much.

We knew what we were there for. After that I went back up to the room and gathered up my luggage and got on the bus to go to the game. We've got a loose group of players, so it wasn't a quiet bus—just like it is during the regular season. We're all professionals and we were treating it like it was any other game. But we knew it wasn't.

I wasn't even thinking about the game. We went in a roundabout way. We should have taken a pack mule the way we were winding around. We went down this road and it seemed like we were going into a riverbed. I was looking at all the beautiful homes up on the hills. I was checking them out, seeing how nice they were.

But once you pull into the parking lot of the Rose Bowl you start thinking about the game. You first see the Rose Bowl when you're about a block away and say to yourself, "Well, that's the place I've heard so much about." Then the whole thing starts getting to you. You know now that you'll be playing in the biggest football game of your life.

Once you get off the bus, things get serious. There isn't any more kidding around. I went straight to the dressing room to be sure things were the way I want them. I want to know where my locker is and then I want to get it organized. I want to have the right number of rolls of tape that I need and I want to be sure I have the right kind of socks. There are two different kinds. I always wear the same kind but not because I'm superstitious. When I walk out on the field I don't want to have to go back because I forgot something like wrist bands.

Some of our players are superstitious. They wear the same clothes to every game. Coach Madden is like that. He wears a brown shirt and brown pants for every game; it doesn't make any difference how cold or hot it is.

Fred Biletnikoff, who always has the locker right next to mine, must tie his shoes 50 times before a game. He'll tie them and then untie them. He'll keep doing it over and over again until they look just right and feel just right.

There are crazy things that happen just before a game. Some guys throw up. I'm not an emotional person so I don't. But some of the other players do.

I'm a soft-drink drinker and I like to have a couple cans of Pepsi right there by my locker.

I make sure my pads feel right and that my knees are taped up the way they should be. I always wear a white sweatshirt under my game jersey and I cut the sleeves off just above the wrists. I want them cut just right so it won't bother me once I get out on the field.

When we walked through a tunnel to the field, I knew I was playing in the Super Bowl. Everybody did and it got real quiet. We were loose but it was quiet.

The first thing I did was to see what condition the field was in. We hadn't worked out there before the game; there had been some rain. I wanted to see if there were any slippery spots.

Next, I located the scoreboard and the clock. There might not be time to start looking for it once the game started. I wanted to be sure I could see the down and distance markers because that's very important to the plays I call. The clock and the scoreboard in the Rose Bowl are easy to read and I was glad of that.

Then I looked for the 30-second clock, the one that tells you how much time you have to run a play. It was kind of hard to find, over a tunnel at the end of the field. I called Gene Upshaw, our offensive captain, over and asked him if he knew where the 30-second clock was.

"Where is it?" he said. There were some people standing up in front of it and it was hard to see.

Next, I checked the sidelines to see if they had the six-foot boundary around them. That way, I can judge where to throw the ball on our sideline passes. Then, just before we went off the field at the end of pregame practice I checked the wind. I wanted to know how hard it was blowing and which direction it was coming from.

As we went off the field, I watched the Minnesota team come on. I wanted to see what their uniforms looked like and how big the players were—guys like Alan Page and Jim Marshall and Jeff Siemon. I had never had a chance to see them in person. Some of them were bigger than I expected; some were smaller, particularly the defensive backs.

I didn't talk to any of their players. I didn't have a chance. But I watched them closely. Sometimes you can tell about a team's attitude just by looking. I couldn't tell a thing about the Vikings.

Once we got back to the dressing room I started thinking about what I would call on the first play. I hadn't really made up my mind because it would depend on where we got the ball. I decide what I'm going to call on the first play and talk it over with the coaches. If they're dead set against it, then I'll call something else.

We're not a fancy team on that first play. We don't try to do anything special. We won the toss and elected to receive. Carl Garrett returned Fred Cox's kick 23 yards to the 34. I had three or four plays in mind when I went out there for the first time. I didn't decide which play I would call until I got down in the huddle. On that first play you just run something straight ahead. You don't want to pull the guards or anything like that. You want everyone just to block straight ahead and get a good hit on someone on the other team. All players are nervous before that first hit of the game.

Once you get that first lick, the butterflies go away. I called a straight-ahead play with Clarence Davis carrying the ball and it gained one yard. Then I called another straight-ahead with Mark van Eeghen carrying and he made four yards. It was third and five and I had my first decision to make.

I wanted to see what Minnesota would do on defense. Sometimes they bring in an extra linebacker or defensive back in passing situations. If they bring in an extra linebacker, we can anticipate a certain defense based on what we saw them do in films. They brought in an extra defensive back so I had a pretty good idea what coverage they would be in. I called a pass play for Dave Casper, our tight end.

That meant their linebacker, Matt Blair, would have to cover Casper man-to-man. That's the kind of situation we were looking for. They did exactly what I thought they would and I threw a pass to Casper that gained 25 yards. Davis gained 4 yards on the next play so I decided to call something special on the play after that. We put it in just for the Super Bowl.

Casper lines up next to Art Shell, the tackle, and they get a double-team block on the left side. That's got to be about four tons of people blocking when you put those two big guys on the same side. Both of them went after Jim Marshall, the defensive end. The program said he weighed about 230 pounds. He didn't look nearly that big and later I found out he went into the game weighing about 219. He never had a chance against Casper and Shell. They buried him.

Van Eeghen is the lead blocker on the play and knocks the linebacker to the outside. Then George Buehler, the guard, pulls and goes through the hole in front of Davis. We manhandled them and Davis gained 20 yards.

The only play I second-guessed myself on all day came just after that. We gained a yard on first down and then I missed on a pass on second down. Everyone in the stadium expected a pass on third down but I decided to get fancy and call a running play. I knew everyone would be looking for a pass, even our trainer, Dick Romanski.

I thought maybe I could pop a run in there and surprise the Vikings and make a good gain. But we didn't fool them. They might have been looking for a pass but they stopped Banaszak on the running play after he gained two yards. That made it fourth down and we went for a field goal and missed. I figured it was my fault we didn't score because of the play I called on third down.

I guess I didn't want to take a chance on an interception. I figured a running play would still put us close enough to get a field goal but then we missed that. But, hell, I still wasn't worried. As I went off the field I got to thinking about the defense Minnesota was using. They were doing exactly what we thought they would, so I knew we could gain yards.

Minnesota is a very basic team. They set their defense and just seem to tell you, "Here we are, come and get us."

I anticipated what they would be doing. Of course,

you can know what defense they are going to be in but you still have to execute. You have to get good pass protection and the receivers have to run the right routes. And then I have to get the ball to them. I didn't do that in our second drive. I missed on a pass that I should have completed to Biletnikoff. We had to punt and Minnesota blocked it and recovered on our three-yard line.

I wasn't concerned at this point. Even if they did score, which they didn't, being behind 7–0 with all that time to play wouldn't have been a big deal. We had proved we can score points in a hurry when we got 17 in the last four minutes of the first game of the season against Pittsburgh.

We got a break when Willie Hall recovered their fumble on the three-yard line. A lot of people seemed to think that the fumble turned the game around. They figured if Minnesota had scored it would have been a different game. It was a big break for us that they didn't score.

We got a good drive going and Davis got loose for 35 yards on one play. We went almost the length of the field. You could tell in the huddle that our people were ready to go. There was no phony chatter. They knew they could move the ball against the Vikings. I didn't think it was going to be easy but I felt confident that we could score. Once we got down near their 20-yard line, they went into a goal-line defense. That's what they always do. They play that short-yardage defense better than any team we played all season.

We had the ball on about the 20-yard line and made six yards on first down. Banaszak made one yard on the next play so it was third and three. I thought back to what I had done in the same situation early in the game where I called a running play in an obvious passing situation. It didn't work. This time I called a pass play. It didn't work either.

We went for the field goal and Errol Mann made it to give us a 3–0 lead in the middle of the second quarter. The first points you get in any game are the hardest and I was happy to be on the scoreboard even if it was only three points.

When I came off the field, Coach Madden was really pissed off. He was hot. He was unhappy that we hadn't taken it in for a touchdown. He thought we should have scored the first time we had the ball, too, and should be ahead 14–0 instead of 3–0.

I told him, "Don't worry, coach. We're going to get a lot more points." He just looked at me and didn't say anything. He was mad. He was ranting and raving and stomping up and down along the sidelines.

The next time we got the ball we started to open up a little. I threw a pass to Cliff Branch on first down and it gained 8 yards to our 44-yard line. Then we ran a couple plays and got a first down. I threw to Branch for 2 yards and then to Casper for 19. Casper is such a great receiver that all you have to do is get the ball close to him and he'll catch it.

The play was a simple little thing where he runs an eight-yard pattern. That gives him a chance to run in their secondary after he catches the ball. Once he does that, he can do some damage. The play worked and he broke one tackle and then ran over a couple other guys. We got a big gain out of it, 19 yards to the Minnesota 26-yard line.

I had Carl Garrett run the ball on the next three plays and he gained 13 yards on the first one, then 4 more and then 3. They weren't the same play. We use so many different formations that we can have the same guy carrying the ball but it will look like something different each time. The Vikings probably didn't figure the same guy would carry the ball three times in a row and it surprised them.

We had the ball with a third down and goal to go on the Minnesota six-yard line. I decided to call a sideline pass to Biletnikoff. He was working on his man pretty good. We knew that down by the goal line they would be in a man-to-man defense. Most of the rest of the time they were in a zone because they didn't want us to complete any long passes. It worked because they played so far back, we couldn't get the ball to our deep men. But down there near the goal line, with not as much territory to cover, they played man to man. That's what we hoped they would do.

When I saw them covering Freddie that way, I knew we could complete the pass. I called a sideline pattern because he is a master at catching that one. All I have to do is give him time to work on his man and then throw the ball close to him. That's what I did and they knocked him out of bounds on the one-yard line.

The next play I called was a roll-out pass to Casper. We had seen other teams do it in films and knew their defense was vulnerable to a play like that. It's a play we worked on all week long so we knew it would work. They came out in the defense I was looking for so I passed to Casper for the touchdown. It was easy.

The next time we got the ball we scored again. The big play was a 17-yard pass to Biletnikoff for a first down on the Minnesota one-yard line. He made a diving catch. The play I called is a story in itself. When we were in the huddle I asked Biletnikoff what he thought he could do—an up pattern or a post. The up is where he goes deep down the sidelines. The post is where he goes to the middle of the field and not as deep. He looked at me and said, "Post." I called, "Far 99 Right, Post, 10 Flat." The last part means the fullback stays in to block to give me more time to throw and the halfback goes out in the flat in case I have to lay the ball off to someone.

We ran the play and Freddie beat his man coming across the middle. The safety man, Nate Wright, came over to help out. He was right on Freddie's tail so I threw the ball where Biletnikoff was the only one who could catch it. If he didn't get it, no one would. I threw a good pass and Freddie came up with his usual spectacular catch. Banaszak took it in for a touchdown on the next play.

As I ran off the field with Biletnikoff I told him, "That was a helluva call on the pass play."

He never ceases to amaze me. When he says he's going to do something you can write it down because he's going to do it.

That put us ahead, 16–0, just before the half but I didn't think the game was won. So many things can happen in a football game that you don't get optimistic too early.

In the locker room, while I had a Pepsi, I went over Polaroids that were taken of the action from upstairs. I talked to the coaches and then Madden told us, "Let's play it like it's 0–0. When we come back here at the end of the game, we'll be the world champions."

I felt better and better as the game went on. Things were going our way and when that happens, we're tough. When things don't go our way and we have penalties and shit like that, we're in trouble.

They got a touchdown on a Fran Tarkenton to

Sammy White pass late in the third quarter and we got a field goal. That made it 19–7 going into the fourth quarter. They got a drive going and had a chance to make a game out of it. But Willie Hall, a guy we had cut in preseason, intercepted one of Tarkenton's passes on our 46-yard line. We made four yards to midfield on two running plays and then I decided to go deep for Biletnikoff.

The Vikings must have blown the coverage. There wasn't anyone covering Freddie and he caught the ball for a 48-yard gain to the two-yard line. He could have scored but they caught him from behind. Biletnikoff will tell you he's not the fastest runner in football. Banaszak took it over and we led, 26–7, after Mann's conversion.

When we completed that pass, I knew we were going to win the Super Bowl. I wasn't thinking about the championship ring or anything like that. I just had a feeling of great accomplishment. I was thinking personally then instead of about the team.

I thought to myself that there are only five or six other quarterbacks who have ever won the Super Bowl and now I was one of them. Usually I think about everything on a team basis but right then I was thinking about myself. I felt a great deal of pressure leave me when I realized we were going to win.

The celebration started even before the game was over. We scored again when Willie Brown intercepted a pass and ran 75 yards. We were on the sidelines laughing and smiling. We weren't laughing at Minnesota. I'll never laugh at another team or player because I know how it feels to be on the losing side. I was there with Biletnikoff and we talked about what good shape we were in—ahead by a big score late in the game.

I don't think Coach Madden was convinced we were going to win even then. I don't know that he's ever convinced until the game is over. Maybe if the score was 48–0 he might be. But I'm sure even he felt pretty good.

There was a helluva story on the sidelines just before the game ended. They announced that Biletnikoff had been named the Most Valuable Player in the game. I was so happy for him. He's played for a long time and I don't know how many years he has left. He's number six or seven on the list of all-time receivers in pro football and then to cap it off by playing in the Super Bowl and being named the MVP! It couldn't happen to a better player on our team.

After they announced the award, Freddie came off the field and started to cry. He's a very emotional person. All the other players were hugging him and shaking his hand. The photographers were taking his picture and the game was still going on. It was really a great experience to see something like that because he deserved it so much.

I walked off the field with a feeling of satisfaction and accomplishment. In the dressing room it was really a madhouse. Everybody was pouring champagne on each other. I felt very happy for some of our players who probably never expected to play in the Super Bowl—guys like Carl Garrett, who was a castoff from another team, and John Matuszak, who got cut by several other teams. And Dave Rose, a journeyman who had been around a long time without getting a chance to play in the Super Bowl.

Willie Hall was cut before the season started and here he was back with us in the Super Bowl. He made some big plays for us. Hubie Ginn is another guy that nobody else wanted, but he helped us.

I was also happy for Coach John Madden and Al Davis. They dedicated their lives to winning the Super Bowl.

It was an emotional scene. I didn't cry but I almost did. I was just kind of gliding along with the whole thing. It's something when you see 250-pound men hugging each other around the neck with tears in their eyes. Big, tough men telling each other how much they love each other, and crying.

Being a part of that is really something but the best part for me was standing back and watching it. I just watched them pour the champagne and celebrate.

Fred Biletnikoff's little boy was in there and he was crying and so was Freddie. It was unbelievable.

It took a while for it to sink in that we had finally won the Super Bowl. I think Pete Banaszak said it the best. "There isn't anyone left to play," he said.

He was right. There weren't any more games. We had beaten everybody.

We had done it all.

2

A Typical Country Boy

Ken Stabler was born on Christmas Day in 1945 in Foley, Alabama, a city of about 4,000 people 20 miles west of Pensacola, Florida, and 8 miles north of the Gulf of Mexico.

Foley is not too close to anything nor is it too far. It is a farm town, but it is also near a beach resort area because of the Gulf. There is a lot happening there for a small place.

I guess you can say my family was lower middle class. My father was a shop foreman for a Chevrolet dealer in town. My mother is a nurse. I did my share by working at odd jobs. In season, I worked at the sheds where they grade produce, stacking potatoes, corn, soybeans, watermelons, or whatever, then crating them in boxcars.

I was a typical country boy and I suppose I didn't

mind raising a little hell. I remember one time when I was in the ninth grade I went off with a few of the guys and stole some hubcaps. When I got caught the next day, I was suspended from school for three days. This happened to be the week of the junior varsity basketball tournament, and while I didn't mind missing my classes, I sure minded not being able to play in the tournament.

As long as I can remember, I've wanted to compete in sports. It didn't matter what game it was. I wanted to play. I started out in Little League baseball where I pitched most of the time and played first base when I wasn't pitching. After that came Babe Ruth League and Pony League.

In football, I played Pop Warner ball and then in the Pee Wee League. My first regular competition was in high school in the ninth grade—on the junior varsity. In my sophomore year I made the varsity. I remember the first game of the season because I didn't get in it. I was upset because of my competitive nature, but later on in the season I got to play and we won every game.

The next year I was the regular quarterback, and we won every game again. We had a great coach. His name was Ivan Jones and he idolized Bear Bryant, the coach at the University of Alabama. He coached like the Bear and our practices were just like they have them at Alabama. I owe a lot to Coach Jones. He got me started in the right direction. I've never been a conformist as far as rules and regulations are concerned, but he straightened me out. It didn't make me change too much but I followed the rules.

There was the time, though, that I was going with this girl I really liked. One day I skipped practice to go over to her house. Sure enough, I got busted.

When the coach got a hold of me the next day he gave me three good licks with a bed slat he used.

I got my first car when I was a sophomore in high school. It was a 1953 Ford. Every day after practice eight or ten of us used to head down to a creek we called the Ice Box because it was so cold. We'd spend the rest of the day skinny-dipping and drinking beer.

My high school career is something I'll never forget. We didn't have a very big school, but we were lucky to have some great athletes when I was there. I was the quarterback. It didn't make any difference that I was left-handed.

That's the only position I've ever played in football and the only one I ever wanted to play. There were some people who were skeptical about me playing quarterback. I never thought of it as a problem. You can't knock success and I've done pretty well as a left-handed quarterback.

My parents and my sister went to all the games when I was in high school. My sister is five years younger than I am and she was pleased to have an older brother who was a big star in football and the other sports. Whenever we played in other places, my mom and dad would go along to watch.

The only game we lost in the three years I was on the varsity at Foley was the first game of my senior year. We played a big school from Mobile, and they beat us, 21–14. But we won two state championships, and I have to say I was fortunate in having such good teammates. You're very close to the guys you win and lose with—the ones you practice with and sweat with. I think of them every now and then, wondering what they're doing now. Some of them went to junior college and some played at four-year colleges. But none made all-conference or anything like that.

I was recruited by quite a few colleges in my senior year. I got letters from them and scholarship offers from all the big schools in the South. I also got offers from the military academies, but I didn't want to go to any of those. The discipline didn't appeal to me.

I decided I wanted to stay in the state of Alabama so that narrowed my choice down to either Auburn or the University. My dad was a big Alabama fan and he used to take me to games when I was in high school. The first one I remember seeing was in either 1959 or 1960. Alabama played Louisiana State in Mobile, and Billy Cannon beat Alabama when he returned a punt for a touchdown.

In the end I settled on Alabama because they were winners. If I was going to bust my ass playing football, I might as well do it for a winning team. And that's what Alabama always was.

Naturally, my father was pleased that I decided on Alabama. He, and my mother, would get to see as many games as they could when I was in college. But my father died just after I graduated from Alabama. He was 47 years old. He never got to see me play in a pro game.

3

Bear

Ken Stabler played four years of football at University of Alabama. He played on the 1964 freshman team, was a reserve quarterback on the 1965 team that had a 9–1–1 record and won in the Orange Bowl; and then was the regular signal-caller on the 1966 national championship team that had an 11–0 record (including a Sugar Bowl victory over Nebraska) and the 1967 team that was 8–2–1 and lost to Texas A&M in the Cotton Bowl, with Ken scoring two touchdowns.

In his last three years at Alabama, Stabler played for Paul "Bear" Bryant, one of the legendary coaches of college football.

Bear Bryant has been the single biggest influence on my life both as a person and as a football player. We had a closeness that has a lot to do with everything I have accomplished in football.

He's a tough guy . . . a tough old bastard. But deep down inside he's got a heart of gold. If you play for him and do what you're supposed to do, give 100 percent every minute you're on the field, even if you don't excel, Bear Bryant will be the best friend you'll ever have.

If I were a kid right now, and I had any kind of a problem, I would go to him.

You name it—dope, women, financial trouble, anything—you just call him and he'll go to bat for you faster than anyone I ever saw. Even when I was out of school, after playing pro football for three or four years, if I had any problem I knew I could call Coach Bryant.

When I was growing up, every kid in Alabama wanted to play for the Bear. He was the reason for their winning tradition. When you play for Alabama in football, it's like playing for the Cincinnati Reds in baseball. You're the best, and there is no doubt about it.

After you're through at Alabama, people still know you. You go back to your small town and you're somebody special because you played for the Bear.

But I had my problems with the Bear. When I was a sophomore I played behind Steve Sloan. He's the coach now at Texas Tech. He was a great quarterback and he led us to the Orange Bowl, but I thought I was better than he was. Coach Bryant didn't agree, I guess, so the only time I played was when Sloan was injured, we had a big lead, or the offense wasn't going too good.

We used the I formation then and the quarterback could run the ball more than in some other formations. We had a very simple offense. It was like when you are working with mules. When we had a play going to the right, I would call "Gee" in the huddle. If we were going to the left, it would be "Haw." Just like when you want a mule to go either to the left or to the right.

In my sophomore year, I passed only 11 times. I completed three for a total of 26 yards. We weren't really a passing team because we had so many good running backs. If an Alabama team threw the ball 15 times a game in those days, that was a lot. I ran the ball 61 times for 331 yards, an average of better than five yards a try. I scored one touchdown.

The next year I was the regular quarterback. We had a great season and won every game we played. I completed 74 of 114 passes for 956 yards and nine touchdowns. And I ran the ball 93 times for 435 yards and scored three times.

We beat Nebraska in the Sugar Bowl, 34–7, to clinch the national championship. I had a good day. I completed 12 of 17 passes for 218 yards and two touchdowns, and ran for 58 yards and another score. I was named the Most Valuable Player in the game and I thought I was really something.

I didn't go to college to study. All I wanted to do was play football and I didn't conform to some of the rules. I wasn't very disciplined and I liked to screw around. But when you played for Bear Bryant, it didn't make any difference who you were or how good you were. If you screwed around and didn't follow his rules, you were gone.

I had problems with Coach Bryant after my junior year. I was running around a lot and he didn't like it. I left him no other choice. People kept telling me if I didn't change my ways, Bear was going to get me.

But I thought I was pretty hot stuff, the MVP in the Sugar Bowl, and a senior coming back for another year as the regular quarterback.

That didn't make any difference. I didn't follow the rules and, bam. I was gone. Suspended.

How did it happen? I hurt my knee in spring practice before my senior year, so Coach Bryant told me to take it easy. He didn't want me to take part in spring practice, but he wanted me around to watch what was going on. He said he had some young quarterbacks he wanted to work with and he just wanted my knee to get well.

But he wanted me at practice and I didn't always show up. I wanted to practice and then I didn't want to. It was very frustrating. I was immature and that was part of it.

I was going with this girl down in Mobile and that was about 250 miles from Tuscaloosa. I started driving down to see her, two or three nights a week. I bought a brand new 1967 Corvette when I didn't have a damn dime . . . not even a nickle. I conned those car people. I told them I was going to be drafted by a pro team and get a big bonus for signing. I was counting on signing with a pro team and then have a lot of money coming in.

So I bought the brand new car and started driving to Mobile to see this girl. The way I would do it was that all the football players had a study hall from seven o'clock until nine every night. Right after nine o'clock, I'd jump in that Corvette and drive to Mobile. It was a four-and-a-half hour drive and I wouldn't get there until one or two in the morning. I'd stay with her for two or three hours, then drive back to school in time for an eight o'clock class in the morning.

I was doing that constantly, and it was rough.

Needless to say, my school suffered and then everything else started to suffer too. After a while, I wouldn't even go to the study hall. I was running around, drinking, not studying and not living up to my responsibilities.

I was the quarterback and the leader of that football team and I wasn't doing the job. I left Coach Bryant no other choice but to suspend me. People kept telling me it was going to happen. But I was hardheaded and cocky. I guess I thought I was too big for him to suspend. I'd always been kind of an individual and done whatever I wanted. It wasn't that I was a prima donna or anything like that, or that I could get away with things. I just didn't care.

Coach Bryant didn't give me any warning. He didn't call me into his office—because I wasn't around. I was down south at home in Foley and he sent me a telegram. It read:

"Ken—you have been indefinitely suspended. Paul W. Bryant."

That's all it said. It didn't bother me too much because I really didn't care. It bothered my folks because my dad was such a big Alabama fan. My parents even did things like having a phony letter sent to me telling me that if I didn't go back to school, I would be drafted into the military service. My dad made up the letter.

It scared me. The only thing I hated worse than going to study hall was the thought of going into the military service. I went back to school. Then some of the young assistant coaches on the football team—Jimmy Sharpe, Pat Dye, and Richard Williamson—got to me and told me I had a helluva future if I straightened out. They told me I had a lot to lose and that Alabama had a chance to win and that they needed me.

Well, I decided to go back to playing football. Bear Bryant didn't seem to care. He figured if I didn't straighten out, he would get someone else to play quarterback. I'm sure he really did care but he didn't want me or anyone else to know that he cared about one player.

I got my grades in order in summer school and everything was OK. I was supposed to get back on the team but I had to go into his office to see him. I walked in and said: "Coach, I'm eligible for football this fall and I'd like to come back."

He said: "I don't give a damn if you are eligible to play football again. I don't care if you want to play or not. I don't think you deserve another chance to play. I don't want you out there."

Can you imagine that? I worked hard to get eligible and that's what Coach Bryant says to me. I told him I didn't care if he wanted me out there or not. I was eligible and I was coming out for the team. He looked at me and finally said: "Son, come back and see me later."

I thought I might get a shot so I went back to see him later. He said I could play football again and the only reason he was letting me do it was because I wouldn't take no for an answer. I guess he had been testing me.

After that, things were pretty good between us.

But when I came out for fall practice, I had to prove to him all over again that I could play football. Hell, it didn't make any difference that I had been the regular quarterback and had been the MVP in the Sugar Bowl. He let me back on the team and that was all. I had to show him I could play.

The first day of practice all the players are assigned to teams. The color of the jersey shows what team you are on. The first team wears red jerseys. The second team wears white and the third team blue. The fourth team is orange and the fifth team is brown. They gave me a jersey and I couldn't even tell what color it was.

I was on the lowest possible team, and I was starting my senior year. There were guys playing ahead of me I had never even heard of. Hell, practice was almost over before I would even get a chance to throw a pass.

When it came time to open the season, I still wasn't the regular. The coach wasn't going to start me no matter what. I had a good fall practice and beat out all the other guys which I knew I would do. But that didn't make any difference to the coach. He did it just for spite, just to let me know he was the guy running the team.

We were two-touchdown favorites over Florida State in the opening game and he started a guy named Joe Kelley, a junior, at quarterback. Kelley was in for only the first series of plays. I don't think he played again that year. I went in for the second series of downs and we ended up playing a 37–37 tie.

After that, I got along very well with Coach Bryant. I learned a lot about conforming to rules and taking responsibilities and making sacrifices for the team.

Now he's very complimentary of me. He said some things through the press and also to some of my friends. He never said things to me directly because that wasn't his way. But we have a closeness, and I know he thinks a lot of me. I think a lot of him.

The suspension helped me because I don't know what would have happened to me if I hadn't changed my ways. I was a wild guy running around. And Coach Bryant straightened me out.

I hear from him. He sends me telegrams during the season. After we beat Pittsburgh in the season opener in 1976, he sent me one congratulating me and wishing me luck in going all the way to the championship.

Another time he sent me one that said: "They finally agree with me that Ken Stabler is the best quarterback I ever coached."

That was really something. Because I'll never forget that first telegram he sent me telling me I was suspended.

Whenever I get a chance, I go back to Alabama and talk football with the coaches. Coach Bryant always gives me a hard time about my long hair. I didn't have that when I played for him. He still treats all his former players as if they are still playing for him. It doesn't make any difference if you're 35 or 40 years old.

Last year this guy was writing a book about winning football, and he called Coach Bryant for a quote. Bear said: "If I could pick one quarterback to win a certain game for me, I would pick Ken Stabler."

Those things mean a lot to me. I know that he likes me now and respects me. And I realize how much he did for me. I wouldn't be where I am today if it hadn't been for Bear Bryant. He taught me a lot, even if I had to learn the hard way.

I still call him when I have problems. There were other times when I should have called him. When I first joined the Raiders, I had problems. My knee was hurt and I was having trouble with my first wife. I was frustrated about not getting a chance to play. I should have called Coach Bryant because he would have settled me down.

I left Oakland and he would have made me stay. I knew what he was going to tell me so I didn't call him. He would have called me an idiot and he would have been right. I feel bad about that because I should have called him.

That's why I say he had the biggest influence on my life as a person and as a football player.

4

Breaking In

Chosen by Oakland on the second round of the 1968 NFL draft, Ken Stabler found himself surrounded by veteran quarterbacks. Daryle Lamonica had brought the Raiders to the Super Bowl the previous season, and his backup was George Blanda, starting his 19th season as a pro. Despite his impressive college credentials, Stabler couldn't expect to crack the starting lineup. But nobody, including Stabler, could have predicted what would happen to him in that rookie year.

When the Raiders drafted me I was happy. I didn't know a lot about the team but I was happy to have a chance to play pro football because that's the only thing I really wanted to do.

The first year in the pros is like the first year of high school or college. You don't expect to play very much but you're still excited about the possibility of getting a chance. But then I hurt my knee and had to have surgery. They had quite a few other quarterbacks so they sent me home and told me to come back the next year.

That was probably a good thing. The Raiders had gone to the Super Bowl the year before (1967 season) with Daryle Lamonica playing quarterback. He was named the Most Valuable Player in the American Conference because he had a great year. And George Blanda had come to the team. He was the backup quarterback. I wouldn't have played much that first season, so maybe it was just as well that I did have the knee operation.

In 1969 I figured I would get a chance. The first game I played for the Raiders was an exhibition against the Dallas Cowboy rookies at Oakland Coliseum. I completed a high percentage of my passes and threw two touchdowns—a pretty good game.

You always wonder just how good you are as you move up to higher levels of competition. It was that way when I went from high school to college. But after that first pro game, things didn't go well for me. My knee was still bothering me and I was having marital problems. I was frustrated on both counts and I thought I should be getting more chances to play.

So I quit for a year. I just went home to get things straightened out in my mind.

Whether it was right or wrong, it was my decision. I have always thought that maybe I should have called Coach Bear Bryant at that time and asked him for advice. But I knew he would tell me to go back to the Raiders and I didn't want to do that. If I had the same decision to make right now, I would do exactly what I did then.

Things have turned out very well for me since then so maybe it was the right decision. When I think back, maybe I wasn't ready to be the regular quarterback for the Raiders in 1969. I was playing behind some very good players. Lamonica and Blanda gave me help and advice. A young player is always in awe of the older players on a team, particularly when they are people like Blanda, Lamonica, and Cotton Davidson. I appreciated the help they gave me, particularly Davidson, another of the quarterbacks.

That's why I go out of my way to help the young quarterbacks who come to us now. I remember how much it meant to me when the veterans helped me in the 1970 season. They helped me, but I still didn't get much chance to play. I hardly played at all. That was the year that Blanda would come into games when Lamonica wasn't moving the team and would do one great thing after another. He won some games for us that I didn't think we had a chance of winning. I got a big thrill out of that season because I held the ball for him on field goals the second half of the season.

I only threw seven passes all year and completed two of them for 52 yards. One was for 33 yards. The next year I came back and it was the same situation. Lamonica was still the number one quarterback and Blanda was backup. All I got to do was hold the ball on extra points and field goals. But I did get a chance to play in some games where we had a big lead. I completed 24 of 48 passes for 268 yards and threw for one touchdown. That was the only year that I have been with the Raiders when we didn't make the playoffs.

Things were just the same when I came back for the 1972 season and it was bugging me. At least, I was moved up to number two quarterback but Daryle Lamonica was having a good season and the Raiders were winning so I didn't play much. We had a 10–3–1 record and I got into about half the games. I completed 44 of 74 passes for 524 yards and four touchdowns.

We played Pittsburgh in the first round of the playoffs in Pittsburgh. That was one of the strangest games I have ever been in. They scored two field goals in the early part of the game and were ahead, 6–0, in the last quarter. Lamonica wasn't having a very good day and neither was Blanda. Finally, Coach Madden put me in. We got a drive going and had the ball down to about their 30-yard line with a minute to play. I went back to pass but couldn't find a receiver who was open. I ran the ball and went all the way for a touchdown. Blanda kicked the extra point and we were ahead, 7–6, with less than a minute to play.

But then they came back with a miracle play when the ball bounced off one of their players and Franco Harris caught it and ran for a touchdown and a 13–7 win.

What a damn frustrating way to end the season. I decided to come back the next year and really work to be the number one quarterback. But things were no better. I got to play in the preseason games and did pretty well. But when we opened the season against the Minnesota Vikings, Daryle Lamonica was still the starting quarterback. We lost the game and I didn't get to play. The next week we bounded back to beat the Miami Dolphins, 12–7, and again I didn't play.

Next we played the Kansas City Chiefs. We were behind, 16–3, late in the game and Coach Madden sent me in for the final five minutes. I had been around for three or four years and the only time I was getting into games was when we were ahead by a big score late in the game or for the last couple of minutes when we didn't have any chance to win. That wasn't very exciting.

I'd had it after the Kansas City thing. I went into Coach Madden's office and told him I didn't want to play in situations like that. I told him if he was going to do that, I would rather play for some other team.

It wasn't a play-me-or-trade-me thing. I felt I was good enough to be the starting quarterback on some other teams in the league and I wanted a chance to do it with the Raiders. Coach Madden said he hated to hear me say that but there wasn't anything he could do about it at that time.

I didn't give up. It was just like when Coach Bryant had kicked me off the team at Alabama and then wouldn't let me come back when I was eligible. I told the Bear I was coming back whether he liked it or not. And I told Coach Madden I wasn't going to quit.

I asked him if I could throw the St. Louis offense the next week. We were going to play the Cardinals in St. Louis and on defense day one of our quarterbacks plays the role of Jim Hart, the St. Louis quarterback, so our defense can see what it looks like. I told him I wanted to be Hart. He said I could and I had a great day. I completed everything I threw against our defense. I was having a great time doing it. I was laughing and joking and having a blast. Madden came up to me after practice and told me I was going to be the starting quarterback against St. Louis.

He said the reason he was doing it was because I didn't quit and that I came out and worked hard to get the job. We won the game in St. Louis, 17–10, and I had a good day. I completed 17 passes, including two for touchdowns. I passed for quite a few yards and after the game they awarded me the game ball.

I've had the starting job ever since. That was the starting point and the whole thing has kind of snowballed since then. I finished the year number two in passing in the American Conference. I had a helluva game against the Baltimore Colts. I completed 25 of 29 passes to break Sammy Baugh's record for the highest pass completion percentage in one game. I threw for three touchdowns and more than 300 yards. It was one of the best games I ever had, and we won.

The only time I haven't been the starting quarterback since then is when I was hurt. I led the conference in passing in 1974 and had 26 touchdown passes. I was named the AFC's Most Valuable Player.

We've been winning ever since. When I think back to when I quit and then decided to come back, I know I made the right decision.

5

Training Camp

The El Rancho Motel is not your typical vacation hideaway. It is just off U.S. 101 in Santa Rosa, California—50 miles north of San Francisco. For 10 months of the year it is the overnight home of weary travelers between Los Angeles and Portland, Oregon. But in mid-July every year, when the temperature gets near the 100 mark, a specialized group of men converges on the El Rancho. They will be there for about six weeks. During that time the number will be reduced. Some will go voluntarily. Others will not. The survivors of the summer ordeal will be the Oakland Raiders of the NFL.

Ken Stabler has been coming to the El Rancho Motel in Santa Rosa ever since his rookie year in 1968. Things have not changed much since that first year. There is always the dream of the Super

Bowl at the start of training camp. And there is always that feeling that only an Oakland Raider could know. Will this finally be the end of the frustration that has kept the Raiders out of the Super Bowl?

The off-seasons have been the same. You can go back three or four years. One year it was a deflected pass off Jack Tatum that knocked us out of everything. And then Miami beats us down there. Another year we gain 29 yards rushing. Last year we go back to play Pittsburgh and it's 10-below weather. We don't get in. It's the same because of what has happened to us in the playoffs. We're picked every year to go to the Super Bowl because we have a lot of talented people. Yet we don't go. Something always happens. Strange things.

I live it over and over again. Why does it happen to us? Why haven't we gone to the Super Bowl?

Granted, we've really gotten a lot further than other people. We're no stiffs. We've been 11–3, 12–2, and seasons like that. There are a lot of teams who would like to be right where we are. But that's not the way it is in pro football. It's all or none.

Look at it two ways. It's frustrating to get that close and then not win. We were 12–2. We got the extra money. We won our first playoff game. We were one game from the Super Bowl. But that still doesn't make it worthwhile. It's the Super Bowl or a bad season. I'm not content with that and the organization isn't either.

Win the Super Bowl or not. You have to live with that. Every year I play and everywhere I go it's the same—Pittsburgh this, and Pittsburgh that. Why do you guys always lose the big ones? That eats on you.

It bothers you. Instead of being a champion and the Super Bowl team you're the guys who can't win the big ones. Howard Cosell says it on TV. You read it in the papers. Is this going to be another year where you guys get to the playoffs and lose?

You have to live with it. That's the bad part about not winning. You're supposed to have to live with it if you don't win. This year is no exception. Every year I've come to camp I've been optimistic because of the people we have to work with. It's a great organization. We have all the tools to win the whole thing. It's been that way for three or four years. I've done a lot of things in the short time I've played. I've won the passing title. I've been a Most Valuable Player. Except one thing. I haven't won the Super Bowl. That's what drives me.

I come back to camp every year. Hey, this is the year I finally get what I want. But something knocks us out of it. Then I come back again. Camp doesn't bother me. I look forward to it, even the two-a-day practices. We stay in camp longer than most other teams. I don't do that much in camp. The thing I enjoy is getting back around football. Getting rolling again. You know, seeing Freddie Biletnikoff and Tony Cline . . . Art Shell . . . Pete Banaszak . . . George Blanda. I enjoy the camaraderie.

I don't say, "Oh, hell, I have to go back to camp." I kind of look forward to camp. Football is not work to me. Practice is not work to me. I want to see the young guys, see what kind of shape everyone is in. Evaluate the whole thing.

Here we are back again. This very easily could be the year. I'm not as optimistic at this point as I was at this time last year because we have some injuries.

That puts the burden on the offense. Or the defense. If they give up points, we have to score.

Five quarterbacks came to the Oakland Raider camp this season. There is Mike Rae, drafted by the Raiders in 1973. He chose to play three years of Canadian football before coming back this season. There is David Humm, the talented lefthander from Nebraska who was the backup quarterback last year. This is his second year with the Raiders. There is Jeb Blount, the tall rookie from University of Tulsa. And then there is the veteran George Blanda.

There is protocol. And some guys have a wait-and-see attitude. There might be some guy who thinks he's going to come in and take your job. He might not want to be that friendly. Any quarterback is a little cocky. I am in my own way. Everyone should be. David Humm is. Mike Rae is. You can't pattern yourself after anyone. Be yourself. Do things your way.

I make a point to say, "Hi, I'm Ken Stabler. How you doing? Glad to have you with us."

It was the first time I had ever seen Blount. Someone introduced us. It was the same with David Humm.

When I first came here, Cotton Davidson, the old quarterback, came over to me. "Anything I can do for you?" he asked.

I'll offer my services. I won't go up to them during a game and say, "Hey, you ought to be doing this or that." I'll say, "I believe if you do this it will help you." I don't try to coach them but I'll help. I like to see them do well.

I have a long-range look at each quarterback.

Which one might take my job and how soon? I don't see it happening too soon. That's the way I feel. I like to get along. I work hard at making guys like me. I want to like them.

I don't want to be the $200,000 quarterback who is way up here and the other guys are down there. I'm no better than guys who dig ditches or pump gas. And they're no better than me. Everyone is equal to me. I'm friendly not because it helps me, but because it helps the team. And because that's me.

6

Born to Be a Quarterback

Ken Stabler was born to be a leader—and a professional football quarterback. It's the only position he ever has played and that's the way he wants it. While he listens to instructions from his coaches and asks for suggestions from his teammates, once the game starts, Stabler is in complete charge.

Maybe the game with the San Francisco 49ers, a preseason game, would mean more to me if I grew up in this area. I know it's a big thing, like the games between Alabama and Auburn where I come from.

The teams, the 49ers and Raiders, make it seem like more than an exhibition game. Some of them treat it like a war. It's players against players, organization against organization, coach against coach. They take it real serious like it means something. But it's nothing special to me. It's the fifth preseason game to get us ready for the regular season. I simply want to do well.

The ones who take it seriously are the fans who go to it or sit in a bar and watch on TV. Or listen on radio. They bet their 10 bucks or their 100 bucks or whatever they bet. Hell, to those guys it's the most important game of the season.

They call it the Bay Bowl. There are people who work in San Francisco but live in Oakland. They want the Raiders to win so they can go to work and tell the ones from San Francisco that Oakland is better than their team. The guy in the bar in San Francisco wants to see the 49ers kick us around even though it doesn't mean anything. And the guys in Oakland want to see us beat the 49ers. It's like the kid who wants to be the strongest or toughest in his neighborhood. That's a big thing but not to me.

We won the game, which was nice, but what I liked about it was the 98-yard touchdown drive we had. That's what football is really all about. That's where a quarterback gets his satisfaction, doing something like that.

I can't remember ever going that far on a drive for a touchdown, not in high school or college. It gave me a good feeling. It wasn't quite like the long drive against the Miami Dolphins in the playoffs last year. That was different. We didn't have to go quite as far but we had to do it in the last minute to win the game.

In the drive against the 49ers, we had 23 plays and it took almost 11 minutes. And I was in control of the whole thing.

How did it feel when we got the ball on our own two-yard line? I looked up the field and it was a damn long way. I don't think any of our players were worried. They're all veterans and have been in that position before. One of the linemen—I think it was George Buehler—said, "We got a way to go but let's do it." That was the feeling of everyone. We know we're capable of scoring from any point on the field. The difference is if it will be on a sustained drive or one play. We can do it either way.

That we did it, even if it did take 23 plays and 11 minutes, proved something for us, even in a preseason game. We had to overcome some penalties and third-and-long yardage situations. A drive like that really can build up your ego. I wasn't planning very far ahead on the drive. When I went into the game Coach Madden had suggested the first play.

I was thinking the same way. When the ball is on your own two-yard line, you don't do anything fancy. We called a very basic play, the fullback going off tackle behind Art Shell and Gene Upshaw.

My first thought was to get the ball out far enough to give our punter a chance to kick the ball. When the ball is on the two-yard line, he doesn't have enough room. He needs about 15 yards and from the two to the back of the end zone is only 12 yards.

We got three yards on the first play so our punter had what he needed. Then I started thinking about getting the first down. After you get a first down you should have a little room so you can open up the offense a little bit. But we only made a couple of yards on second down. The 49ers were really dug in because they knew we were going to run the ball. Our guys just couldn't knock them out of there so I knew I was going to have to throw the ball.

I threw a safe little pass to Mark van Eeghen, the fullback, and we got the first down, so then I could start thinking about some other things. We completed a couple more passes and that put the ball out near midfield. Then we started to open up. We completed eight passes in the drive. I had a lot of fun. Once having some room to operate, I enjoy trying to outguess the defense.

As soon as each play is over I look at the sidelines to see what the down and distance is. That pretty much decides what you are going to do on the next play. Sometimes the plays just pop into your head. I'll look over at the down marker and right away, I'll know what play I'm going to call. If I look over and it's third and eight, I'll pass. That doesn't take any thinking. That's just what you have to do.

What I will do is start thinking what pass will work in that situation. Other times I'll go back to the game plan and try to remember if there is something that we could use. We can anticipate what kind of coverage the defense will be in and then call something to take advantage of it. I'll watch their defense all through the game to see what they do in different situations. If I see them go into a zone defense against a certain play, and I expected them to be in man-to-man, I'll file that away for later in the game.

If I think I'm going to see some other kind of coverage and I get it, then I'll file that away too. Those are the little things a quarterback has to be aware of all through the game. It's a chess game between me and the guy who calls the defensive signals. He tries to guess what I'm going to do and I do the same with him. If I guess right, we win the game. If I don't, we lose. It's as simple as that.

That's what I enjoy about playing pro football. I like being on the field, calling the plays, having complete control of what's going on, and that's the way it was in the 98-yard drive against the 49ers.

There isn't much talking in the huddle. We have an experienced team and I think the other players trust my judgment. A few years ago, when Daryle Lamonica was the quarterback, it wasn't that way. He would come into the huddle and ask the other players what he should do. They didn't have confidence in him.

I don't ask the other players what we should do. I'll ask them if they think a certain play will work but that's all, and I won't do it in the huddle. I'm open for suggestions because those guys in the line know what they can do. They know how they can handle the guy playing across the line better than I do. I listen to those suggestions. If one of them says he needs some help on a block against a really tough opponent, I'll make sure that he gets it.

We have guys who want to call the plays for me. The wide receivers are like that. Cliff Branch thinks I should throw the ball to him on every play. He begs for the ball. We'll be walking back to the huddle and he'll say, "I can beat my man on a bend-up" or "I can beat my man on a post pattern. He thinks he can beat his man on every play and he's probably right. But I can't throw the ball to him all the time. He knows that.

Sometimes I can tell when Cliff really wants me to throw to him. He'll repeat, "Snake, I can beat my man, I can beat my man." If it's a situation where I think I can get the ball to him, I'll do it. But I'm the one who calls the plays.

It's just the opposite with Fred Biletnikoff, our other starting wide receiver. He won't say anything. He might go through the whole game without saying a single word in the huddle. I talk to him on the sidelines. I ask him what he thinks will go. He'll say he can beat his man on a corner pass so I file that away.

Fred has been around and he knows what plays will work against certain teams or players. But he doesn't say anything. I have to ask him. I never have to ask Branch. When I ask for suggestions from the linemen, it will be about a certain play. I already have an idea what play I'm going to call. I want to know if they think it will work.

I'll ask Buehler if he thinks he can get a trap block on his man. I'll do it as we're walking back to the huddle. Then, if he thinks it will go, I'll call it in the huddle. It isn't a democracy. When we get in the huddle, I'm the one in charge. Everyone on our team knows who is running the show. That's the way it has to be.

It can't be any other way and I wouldn't want it to be. I don't think I could play quarterback on a team where the coach sent in all the plays. I don't think I could play any other position except quarterback either. I've never given it a thought because I've been a quarterback from the time I was big enough to pick up a football.

I like having the responsibility. I like to have people depending on me. It makes me feel good to have a third down and 15 yards to go and complete a pass for the first down. I like to have people tell me I did a good job after something like that.

I like the pressure of being the quarterback. Pressure bothers some players more than it does others. I enjoy it. I think it brings out the best in a football player; at least it does for me. I liked what I was doing on the long touchdown drive because there was pressure all the way. First, there was the pressure to get us room to kick the ball. We did that. Then, there was pressure to get the first down. And we did it.

The most pressure of all was to get the touchdown after going all the way. Hell, it would have really been bad to have the ball that long and go all the way and then not score a touchdown.

There was pressure on me to call the right plays. I could call 10 right plays in a row and then one bad one would kill the whole thing. That's why I wasn't trying to think too far ahead. A quarterback has to wait to see what happens on each play.

It can work two ways: Suppose you call a running play and then plan to call another on the next play. The first play loses yards. Now you have to do something else. Or suppose you have the ball on your opponents' 20-yard line and you call a running play and it gains a big chunk, down to the 3-yard line, for example. You're going to be thinking about calling a different play when the ball is on the 3-yard line than you are if it's on the 10 or 15.

We've got a lot of plays in our offense so I'm never worried that we won't have something to call. We've got 25 or 30 pass plays and about the same number of running plays. We can run each of those plays from three or four different formations. That makes each play different and it gives us a total of more than 200 plays.

That's what I like about playing for the Oakland Raiders. We have a very flexible offense. We can do almost anything we want. You can take guys and put them here or there on the field. I feel like a kid with an erector set. Or like playing electric football.

I can put Cliff Branch on either side of the field or I can put him in the slot. I can put him anywhere I want.

Our offense has proven to be a good one over the years. We always have winning seasons, we make a lot of yards passing, and we score a lot of points. I think the fans enjoy watching us play.

I don't have that much to do with the actual game plan each week. The coaches do that based on what they see in the films. They know what will work against certain teams. I don't watch films unless I have to. I'll watch them in the meetings but that's all. I never take a film home and watch it like some quarterbacks do. I have always believed that if you get ready for a game in practice, you don't have to watch films.

You know there are certain things you can do to neutralize what the other team does best. Against the 49ers we knew we had to do something to slow down Cedrick Hardman, their defensive end. He's a great pass rusher. We put in some plays just for him. We had a pass where we let him come and then toss the ball over his head. We had another play where we use the tight end to cut him down when he isn't expecting it.

On our team it comes down to what the quarterback wants to do. It's that way at least 95 percent of the time with the Raiders. I can't imagine it being any other way. I enjoy the responsibility of being the leader.

That's why I'm the quarterback.

7

Life with Blanda

When Ken Stabler was born, George Blanda was playing freshman football at the University of Kentucky.

Thirteen years later, when Stabler was playing junior high school football in Foley, Alabama, Blanda had completed the first phase of his pro grid career with the Chicago Bears. That year, 1959, Blanda was dropped by the Bears because he was too old and did not fit into their future plans.

Then, in 1967, after an up-and-down career with the Houston Oilers, Blanda was traded to the Oakland Raiders. He helped them win the American Football League championship and a trip to the Super Bowl in Miami's Orange Bowl against the Green Bay Packers.

Stabler, a senior at the University of Alabama,

was playing his final college game that very same week against Texas A&M in the Cotton Bowl in Dallas, Texas. The next season Stabler was drafted by the Raiders and joined the team in training camp where he met George Blanda, the living legend.

I always had a lot of respect for George Blanda because he's been playing football as long as I can remember. There aren't many guys who can play pro football when they're in their 40s and George was 40 when I first met him. He's respected by everyone. He's like a good bottle of wine. He just seemed to get better and better as the years went by.

He had those super years in 1970 and 1971. That was some of the most exciting football I ever saw. He won all those games almost by himself and I was holding the ball for his extra points and field goals then.

I'll never forget the first time I held the ball for him. It was in the 1970 season and we were playing the Cleveland Browns. We were seven points behind with only about three or four minutes to play. Then Blanda came in. He got us a touchdown in about two minutes and tied the score after he kicked the extra point.

He had taken over for Daryle Lamonica, our regular quarterback, who got hurt. Lamonica also was the holder on extra points and field goals. When he couldn't play, I got the job. I held the ball on the extra point that tied the game and I thought, "Well, that's it. At least we tied these guys."

But Blanda didn't feel that way. We got the ball back again and Blanda went to work. He completed a couple passes and got the ball back up to midfield.

There were only a few seconds left. I went in the game and held the ball for him and he kicked a field goal of about 50 yards and we won, 23–20.

I was jumping up and down I was so excited. But not old George. He just trotted off the field in those little choppy steps of his. Hell, he's been through that kind of situation 100 times before. It wasn't exciting to him. If it was, he didn't show it.

He did that kind of thing for us several times that year. I've never seen a player dominate a season like Blanda did for us that year. It seemed like every time we needed a miracle to win a game, there was Blanda doing it.

I held the ball for him for the next six years. His locker was right next to mine, so I got to know him very well. We were two of a kind. We liked the good life so we socialized off the field. I probably got to know him better than the other players. A lot of our players thought George was cranky and I guess he could be. He had a short fuse and he always said exactly what he thought. It didn't make any difference who he was talking to or what they thought.

I remember once a reporter asked him how come he missed a field goal. George looked at him and said, "I just missed the fuckin' thing. I've missed them before and I'll miss them again."

Then he just walked away.

I always liked George's honesty. We got along very well. He never told me I threw a terrible pass even when I did. He would say, "If you had done this instead, it would have been better." That's the way he was with people he liked.

He never really pushed himself on me. He'd been around all that time but he never tried to tell me how I should play. George wouldn't be around people he didn't like. So I know he liked me. I listened to him because I thought he was a messenger for Al Davis, the Oakland Managing General Partner. Al would talk to George because he knew that if George did tell me something, I would listen to him. I never really understood why Al did that. I would have listened to Al directly.

George Blanda helped me with the things I should do and also with the things I shouldn't do. That's where his experience helped. He had been around. He'd seen it all and I was just a young player. He was always there . . . like a force that would settle you down when you needed it. At least that's the way it was for me. I don't think he did that with many other players.

He didn't really have to say anything. Just having George around seemed to give everyone a good feeling. When things weren't going well for me—and they weren't early in my career with the Raiders—Blanda was always there as a support.

I had heard of George when I was a little kid. Hell, I was 3 years old when he started his pro career with the Bears. When I was 10 or 11 years old, I knew who George Blanda was. Kids knew all about the pro football stars and Blanda was one of them. When I was about 13, my father took me to Mobile, Alabama to see an exhibition game between the Houston Oilers and the New York Titans. Blanda was playing for Houston.

After the game, I waited outside the dressing room and got Blanda's autograph. When I came to the Raiders a decade or so later, I told him about it and we laughed. But I got the feeling it wasn't really that funny to him. One thing about Blanda, he didn't like to be reminded about how old he was.

It was still funny. Here I was playing on the same team with a quarterback who had given me his autograph when I was a little kid.

I think it's an honor to have played on the same team with Blanda. That's one part of my career I'm happy with. He's an exception to every rule there is.

I was aware of what was going to happen to him this season and I think he was too. I couldn't have said there was someone who was going to come along and take his place but I know the Raiders were thinking about the future. They had to make some long-range plans and Blanda was 48 years old.

They drafted Fred Steinfort real high and when they do that you know that player is going to get every chance to make the team. The handwriting was on the wall for Blanda.

He had been here with the Raiders every year that I have been here. He came here in 1967 and I started in 1968. It's kind of strange to look around and not see George kicking the ball on the other practice field. Even after he was gone, I would look over at the other practice field and expect to see him.

I think it was great what he did. The best part of his career came at the end and that's the way it should be. He finally got his reward for all those years he put in with the Chicago Bears and the Houston Oilers. He was with the Bears for 10 years and really didn't get that much chance to play. That's a whole career for a lot of players.

Then he went to Houston and played in a couple of championship games. He had a couple of rough years there when the fans got after him. But then he came to the Raiders. He's had three careers, three different careers. It's amazing that anyone lasted as long as he did. He got kind of moody toward the end. He can be very temperamental but I think that's partly because he's so competitive.

George thought he was better than any other quarterback we had. There wasn't any game he played—off the field or on—where he didn't think he was better than you were. That's one thing he always had going for him. I know from just some of the small things that happened. When I first joined the Raiders, I used to play gin rummy with George on our charter flights. I happened to beat him one time and he wouldn't talk to me for the rest of the flight. It was no big thing. We were playing for a penny a point. But Blanda didn't like to lose no matter what he was playing.

Anything he did he was good at. You name it. He could play it. He's a good golfer, a good bowler, a good card player. He's even a good basketball player.

He loved to gamble. He would bet on anything. He would bet you he could beat you at anything and he would usually do it. I've never known anyone with competitive spirit like he had. When he was out on the field, he acted like he was 25 years old. He never wanted anyone to feel he was as old as he was. I admired him for that. But when it got near the end, he stayed away from everyone, even those of us who were his good friends. He acted like everyone else knew he was going to get cut and they stayed away from him. It was almost like he had a terminal illness. People just seemed to stay away from him.

I know the older players didn't feel that way. Fred Biletnikoff, Pete Banaszak, and I, who had known him over the years, tried to keep things the same as they had always been. When he finally did get cut, he just left. He didn't bother to say goodbye to the guys who had been his friends. That was just his way. I didn't think he wanted it to be embarrassing for him or us. So he just left.

But I know I'll see him again because he'll come back to California. We talked just before he left but before he was told he had been cut. I knew what his feelings were. He didn't want to go to another team. I honestly believe he just wanted to be put on waivers. It was sad, in a way, the way it happened. But he's had a hell of a career and has been rewarded for everything. I had mixed emotions about the whole thing.

I don't think the Raiders handled it the right way. They wanted Blanda to retire and go out gracefully the way Jim Otto did the year before. But George didn't want it that way. He wasn't going to quit on his own. You would have to pack up his equipment and hide it. Then tell him he had been cut. That's the only way it could be. He wasn't going to throw in the towel. He was going to keep plugging until they told him he was cut.

In a serious moment he told me once he would never retire. He said they would have to take his uniform away from him.

I remember a funny story about him quitting. It was several years ago after a playoff game against Pittsburgh. We got beat, like we always seemed to do against them, and everyone was dejected and sitting in the locker room after the game.

It was real quiet. Nobody was saying anything. We were taking off our uniforms. I took off my football shoes and put them in front of my locker. An equipment boy came along and asked if he could pack them. I told him he could.

George put his shoes on the floor and the equipment boy asked if he could take them. But George said no.

"Leave those shoes right there," George told the kid. "Leave those shoes right there because that's probably the last football game they will ever play."

There was a pause and then he slapped me on the leg.

"The last game this year," he added.

There was some humor in Blanda although not many people had a chance to see it. He didn't like to needle people but he could laugh at others and he didn't mind if you laughed at him—as long as there was something to laugh about. You didn't laugh at him otherwise.

He liked to joke around and be one of the guys. You know how athletes are. He was right in there giving guys a hard time and he took his licks in return. He even made a joke about it when he finally got cut. He said the Raiders called all the players out on the practice field and then Coach Madden said, "All right, you guys who are still with the Oakland Raiders, take one step forward . . . Not so fast there, Blanda."

But it really wasn't funny for him at the end. It hurt him the way it was done, although he didn't show it. Maybe hurt isn't the right word. I think he was more disappointed than hurt. He didn't want to leave when the time came. He would have played until he was 80 if they had let him.

He talked about maybe being a coach when he quit playing. There were times when offers came along, like the Tampa thing. Every time a coach got fired he would talk about it, like maybe he was interested in the job. He would say he would consider being a coach but it would have to be his way. He would have to be in complete control. It had to be the right situation for him and I guess it just never came along.

I've never met anyone like him. And I never expect to see anyone like him again. He's a sports legend. He was always the same. Even when he missed a field goal. He hated it. It was just like anything else in his life. When he did something, he wanted to do it right.

George hated crybabies and excuse makers. I know where he got that—from Bear Bryant. Blanda played for Bryant when the Bear was coach at Kentucky. Bryant always said: "Never make an excuse, take the blame or take the praise. But don't make excuses." He always said to take the glory whenever you deserve it and take the criticism whenever you deserve that.

If Blanda missed a field goal, he never blamed it on me. He never said I didn't hold the ball the right way. If it wasn't a good hold, he knew that I knew it and he didn't have to tell me. And when it was a perfect hold and he missed, he would just trot off the field. He didn't act any different if he made it or missed it. If he missed one, and I went over to him, he would tell me what he did wrong. If it was his fault, he would say he took a wrong step or that he was too far to one side. He always knew exactly what he did wrong when he missed.

If it was a bad snap from center, that was something else. He would find the center and chew him out. He felt that was not giving him a chance to do his job. Or if a lineman missed his block and someone got through to mess up the field goal, Blanda wanted to know whose fault it was. Then he would find the guy and chew him out.

He wanted things to be right. I've seen him really jump on people if they did something wrong. It didn't make any difference if it was a rookie or an all-pro like Gene Upshaw. If someone didn't do his job, Blanda let them know about it. I guess he's like Bobby Layne in that regard. That's what they say Layne used to do if someone did something wrong.

Blanda was an interesting guy just to be around. You could listen to the stories he would tell all day—about the old days with Johnny Lujack and Sid Luckman and George Halas of the Chicago Bears.

Blanda had quite an effect on my career. He helped a lot when I first came to the Raiders. The first year I got hurt and had to have a knee operation. And I had some other personal problems. Then when I came back in 1970 and 1971 I sat on the bench. I wasn't happy. I was discontented because all through my career I had played and I didn't like to watch.

Maybe I was ready to play then and maybe I wasn't. I know I thought I was ready and that's why I was unhappy. All athletes feel that way. Finally I got so upset I went to Al Davis and asked to be traded. I thought that was the only way I could get a chance to play. I really didn't care where I went. All I wanted was a chance to play.

That's when Blanda took me aside. He calmed me down. He told me to study and work hard and be ready when my chance did come. He told me that a chance might only come once and I had better know what the hell I was doing when mine came. He said I had to take advantage of it. That made me feel more comfortable. I did work hard and I was ready to play when the chance did come early in the 1973 season.

I have to give George Blanda the credit for making sure I was ready. Maybe if I hadn't listened to him I would be playing somewhere else now and not doing as well. George was that way with a lot of guys. He didn't make a big thing of it. He was a good influence. If someone was doing something that was out of line, George would let him know about it.

I'm not sure what effect it will have on me now that he's not here anymore. I don't think it will make as much difference now than it would have if it had been earlier in my career. I'm older and experienced. I've seen lots of things in football but I don't think I've seen it all. It's a continuous learning process and I learned from Blanda.

Maybe now I can have the same effect on some of our young players. I hope I can.

He was kind of a foundation that we built on. That happens when you have a 48-year-old guy playing for you. Right now I still expect him to walk in sometime and start telling people what to do.

He'll be missed. I'll miss the friendship with him and Pete Banaszak and Tony Cline.

I'll miss the five-handed poker games we used to have at the Hilton Hotel the night before our home games. George would come down to my room and then the other guys would come by. It got to be a superstition. We thought if we didn't play poker every week, we wouldn't win. We won every week so we kept playing cards . . . the same guys.

We all liked to do things together, play cards, gamble, have a few drinks. We were all birds of a feather, good-time Charlies.

I'm glad I had a chance to know George Blanda. It won't be the same without him.

8

The Steelers Feud

For as long as the players can remember, there has been a bitter rivalry between the Oakland Raiders and the Pittsburgh Steelers.

No one is quite sure how it started. But it is very real. They are natural enemies—like the cobra and the mongoose, the hawk and the field mouse, or the shark and smaller fish in the sea.

Unfortunately for the Raiders, they usually played the role of the cobra, the field mouse, or small fish when they met the Steelers.

And now, the 1976 NFL season will start with another renewal of the feud—this time at the Oakland Coliseum on September 12.

It isn't one of those phony newspaper rivalries. Our players don't like them and they don't like us. How would you feel if someone picked your pocket every year? For $25,000. They've knocked us out of the playoffs a few times and we knocked them out once. There's always talk about dirty football. But we don't do anything they don't do. Their players kick you when you're down. They'll step on you if you give them the chance.

As soon as the schedule comes out during the off season, you look to see who you play. And there it was—Pittsburgh in the opening game of the regular season.

You go through the six exhibition games and they don't mean a damn. And all of a sudden it's Pittsburgh. How can we forget what they did to us in the past? How can we forget the game where Franco Harris caught the deflected pass in the last minute and beat us? That's the kind of games we always play with them—one controversy or another.

In 1975 there was the frozen field in Pittsburgh. I'm not saying they did that on purpose but there was a cover over the field to keep it from freezing and then it got torn during the night. That field was like rock. We may not have beaten them if the field hadn't been frozen but I think they played better on it than we did.

It's become a helluva rivalry. We think about the Steelers even if we don't play them during the regular season. We know we'll probably have to play them in the playoffs. We know we have to beat them if we want to go to the Super Bowl. They're the reason why we haven't been to the Super Bowl. That eats on you.

But nobody talked about the Pittsburgh game the week before. There was none of that rah-rah stuff. We tried not to think of it as a grudge game because we were sure we could beat them if we played well.

I always look at the mood of our whole team before

a game. I can usually tell how we're going to play. We had quiet confidence. There wasn't anyone saying we had to beat the Steelers. No one had to. We also realized that it was just 1 game in 14. If we lost to Pittsburgh, it wasn't the end of the year. We could still get in the playoffs.

But everyone knew how nice it would be to open by beating the Steelers. We know we're good enough to beat any team we play. And that includes Pittsburgh. We could play their kind of football. We could hammer them. Or we could throw the ball. We knew what we had to do and I knew we could win.

I got our game plan on Wednesday. My first thought was that we had too much stuff . . . too many plays. I didn't think we would ever use that much. We had too many pass patterns because we really didn't expect to throw the ball as much as we did.

I was happy with the running plays. They were good and there weren't too many. We're pretty basic in our running plays. We think our offensive line can open a hole against any team in the NFL. I knew exactly what we wanted to do with our running game and I was confident we could do it even though the Steelers had the best defense in pro football.

But I wasn't sure of the passing game. We have a very sophisticated passing game. I thought, "Hell, I'll never be able to remember all those plays." In the course of the game, we used all the plays we had in the game plan. And I remembered them all. I didn't plan on throwing 38 or 40 passes against Pittsburgh. But that's what I did. I've always felt that you could beat Pittsburgh if you throw the ball 40 times. I knew what I needed was the time to throw.

The first time we had the ball I completed a couple of passes—one to Dave Casper the other to Carl

Garrett—and we got the ball down to their 30-yard line. I probably should have kept on throwing but we ran two plays and didn't gain anything. I missed on a pass to Morris Bradshaw so we went for a field goal and missed.

It was no big deal. I felt there were some things we could do against the Steelers. We got a drive going again the next time we had the ball and got to their 14-yard line but then I threw a pass to Cliff Branch in the end zone and Glen Edwards intercepted.

We scored the next time we had the ball. I really felt good because every time we had the ball we had been able to move. Our defense was doing a good job and I had a good feeling about the game. They got a touchdown just before the half to tie the score.

They really came after us in the third quarter. I had two passes intercepted and they scored after the second one to go ahead, 21–7. We scored on a diving catch of a pass by Fred Biletnikoff, but then they came right back and scored to make it 28–14 with about six minutes to play.

The next time we got the ball they intercepted another pass and I started to think it wasn't going to be our day. But then we got a break and recovered a fumble as they were driving for a touchdown that would have won the game.

I figured the only way to get points in a hurry was to throw the ball so I threw it. I completed four passes for 72 yards on a scoring drive of 75 yards. That made it 28–21 but there were less than three minutes to play.

They got the ball again but our defense held and Warren Bankston partially blocked a punt and we had the ball on their 29-yard line. That gave us the break we needed.

When you get into a situation that we were in, where we had to score in a hurry, you don't do something special. You go with the things you do best . . . the bread-and-butter plays. And our bread-and-butter is throwing the ball to people like Branch and Biletnikoff.

Why abandon things that you know can win for you? You don't play a whole season and then do something different when you get in the playoffs. Sure, there are some new plays but you always come back to the things you know will work.

I've always been a firm believer in doing what you do best when you get in a critical situation. And our situation with Pittsburgh was critical. We could have lost the game very easily there at the end. I really didn't know how close Mean Joe Greene came to getting me until I saw the films after the game. I knew when I ducked that he came awfully close to sacking me. And if he had, that would have been the game. It would have been over right there.

It was fourth down. I wasn't thinking about what would happen if I got sacked because I didn't plan to have that happen. All I was thinking about was avoiding the rush. Then I started thinking about completing the pass. I had to find a receiver.

I was moving to the left when Greene chased me and that was good because that's the way I like to go when I throw.

My concentration was on trying to find a receiver on the left side of the field. That's where Cliff was, so I pretty much ignored everyone else and tried to get the ball to him. I didn't have time to look for anyone else. The idea is to find someone, anyone, who is open and past the first-down marker.

When the play started, it was fourth and 10 to go

on the Pittsburgh 29. There was about a minute and a half to play and we were losing, 28–21. After I ducked under Greene, I saw Cliff. He was in the clear. All I had to do was get the ball to him because I knew he would catch it. When he saw I was in trouble, and scrambling, he did the same thing. His job is to find an open spot and then look for the ball. He knew he had to be past the first-down marker.

A lot of credit goes to Branch. He found an open lane across the middle of the field. With his speed, no one could keep up with him. Branch made a good catch of the pass and almost got into the end zone. Mike Wagner caught him on the two-yard line. The play took almost half a minute so we only had about one minute left. I figured I would call a play that didn't take much time.

I took a time out and talked to Coach Madden on the sidelines. We were both thinking about the same play to get the touchdown—a rollout to the left with me carrying the ball. I got good blocking and scored. Now it was 28–27. We still needed another point to tie.

We had a rookie kicker—Freddie Steinfort from Boston College. I thought how much pressure there was on a kid like that and what he was thinking about. The game is over if he misses it. We had done our job and we still didn't have a tie. You're not completely relieved until he kicked that point.

I remember coming off the field and saying to someone: "Jesus, if that kid misses the extra point, everything we did was in vain." You can't really relax until you look up and see that 28th point on the scoreboard.

I've held the ball on extra points. I know how many things can go wrong so maybe that's why I was a little more worried than I should have been. But the kid made it. That was a great pressure performance by a rookie in his first NFL game.

With the score 28–28 and a minute to play, I honestly didn't think we would get the ball again. I thought Pittsburgh would call some safe plays or just sit on the ball and then take their chances in overtime. Then I thought they might try to go for a long pass to get the ball close enough to kick a field goal from midfield. It would have been a long, long field goal but I figured they might try for it if they could get the ball up near midfield. Then, if they missed, the game would go into overtime.

I was on the sidelines with the coaches when Pittsburgh got the ball. I was thinking about what I might do if we did get the ball one more time. The coaches were talking about it too. We figured if we did get the ball, it would probably be out near midfield. I wanted to know what formations we would use . . . three wide receivers or what. I never really thought we would get the ball down as close as we did. I don't think anyone expected that.

Then Terry Bradshaw tried to throw a pass and Willie Hall, our linebacker, deflected the ball and caught it before it hit the ground. That was a great play. As I ran on the field, I knew what I was going to do. The coaches had reminded me we had two time outs left so I could stop the clock when I had to.

We got the ball on the Pittsburgh 12-yard line and there were 50 seconds left. In the huddle I was thinking about a safe play to call. I also had to remember to keep the ball right in front of the goalposts so the kicker wouldn't have to try a field goal from an angle. I told the ball-carriers to be sure they had the ball when I gave it to them. I told them that Pittsburgh would be grabbing at them, trying to get the ball away. I told them it didn't make a damn if they gained any yards or not. All they had to do was hold onto the ball.

But our ball-carriers, Pete Banaszak and Mark van Eeghen, are experienced. I didn't have to tell them. I just wanted to remind them. It didn't make any difference if we didn't score a touchdown. We just wanted that chance to go for the field goal. I wasn't going to get fancy. I called the first play while time was out and we were ready to go when the clock started after the change of possession.

The play was East Far Right, 65, Lead Man. That's a very basic play. It's a handoff to the fullback with the halfback blocking for him. In this case van Eeghen was blocking for Banaszak. The play is supposed to be run between our left guard and left tackle—Gene Upshaw and Art Shell. Banaszak made three yards and then their linebacker, Jack Lambert, tackled him. The ball was on the nine-yard line and we had 45 seconds left. I figured I could call another play without taking a time out.

This time it was East Far Right, 69, Lead Man. That's almost the same as the first play I called. Banaszak carries the ball but he can run any hole he can find. He doesn't have to run to the left side. He went to the right and made five yards before Lambert tackled him again.

There were 21 seconds left so I called a time out. I really should have let the clock run a little longer before calling the time out. But I guess you get cautious. You don't want anything to go wrong. If I had let the clock run down a little more, Pittsburgh wouldn't have had a chance to run those two plays at the end of the game. They still had a chance to win.

I wasn't worried about Steinfort making the field goal. I knew that even if he missed, we would still have a chance in sudden death. It wasn't like the extra point. That was the one he had to make.

He made the field goal and we won, 31–28.

I've never been in a game where we were that far behind against such a good team and then came back to win.

A lesser team might have quit when it was as far behind as we were that late in the game. But we had been through all that sort of thing before. In the playoff game against Miami a year ago, we were behind after half a minute when they returned the opening kickoff for a touchdown. Then we were still behind with a minute to play and went the length of the field to score a touchdown and win.

There wasn't any dirty stuff done to me during the game. I like to be friends with the people I play against, even the Pittsburgh Steelers. I talked to their players during the game. When they would sack me or knock me down after I threw the ball, I would say, "Nice play." I did it when Joe Greene knocked me down several times and then helped me up. That's the way football should be. And I did it when Ernie Holmes knocked me down.

I remember when I completed a pass for about 30 yards after they put a big rush on me. I said to Greene, "How did you like that one?" He smiled at me. Then, one time I ran a sprint-out and it was real close whether I went over the line of scrimmage before I threw the ball. I completed it to Dave Casper for a first down. Joe Greene and Ernie Holmes were screaming at the official. "He's over the line, he's over the line of scrimmage," they were yelling.

I was standing by Greene and laughing. Then I

winked at Joe and said: "It was close, wasn't it?" Then I walked back to our huddle.

You have to enjoy it out there or you shouldn't be playing the game. It's just like Chuck Noll, the Pittsburgh coach, says: "It's a tough, damn game."

Later he accused us of dirty play because of what George Atkinson did to Lynn Swann. I don't see how he can say that after what one of their players did to Branch earlier in the game. He threw him down on top of his head.

That's the way I see it, and I'm being as honest as I can. I've seen film clips of Pittsburgh doing all the same things they accuse us of doing. I'm not saying what they do or what we do is right or wrong. I'm only saying that they do the same things we do and Chuck Noll knows it.

Guys play emotionally because this is their bread-and-butter. They don't like to lose and sometimes they will do things that are against the rules to keep from losing. I've seen Pittsburgh players do things that are absolutely against the rules. I've seen them kick guys on purpose. I've seen them step on guys when they are on the ground. I've seen their players kick other players in the back and they know that's illegal. But Pittsburgh players do it.

It's a tough damn game but it doesn't have to be a dirty game.

After we beat Pittsburgh, I felt like we had won the championship. I've never won a championship, at least not yet, but it was a very rewarding feeling. We had beat the team that won the Super Bowl the year before. They were the World Champions and we beat them.

That night I went out and had a few drinks and just reminisced about the game. I was with Pete

Banaszak and his wife and my wife. The only thing Pete and I could talk about was what players always talk about after something like that. What a great win it was.

I kept thinking about the things I had done and the things I hadn't done—like throw all those interceptions. Then I got to thinking about plays I called in short-yardage situations and if they were right. And I thought about the times I had receivers open and didn't get the ball to them. Or times when I didn't even see a receiver who was open.

But, hell, we won the game and afterward it didn't make any difference how we did it.

We went out to dinner, Pete and I and our wives, to The Grotto, a fish restaurant in Jack London Square. I like to get out and get around and talk to people, have drinks and buy drinks and all that stuff. I know when I go to The Grotto the owners take good care of us. We patronize the place because the owners are such good football fans. We don't get any special treatment and that's the way it should be. Our money spends just like anyone else's. We take whatever table happens to be open.

I don't usually order anything special when I go there. I like everything they have because I love seafood and that's what they serve. I like abalone, petrale sole, and all kinds of fish. That night I had scampi, those big shrimp served with garlic sauce. I told Pete Banaszak I would eat scampi for 14 weeks in a row if it meant we would win all our games.

I had scampi and scotch. I'm a scotch drinker ... Johnny Walker Red Label. Just like Joe Namath. Our quarterback coach, Tom Flores, drinks scotch too. Sonny Jurgensen drinks scotch. Maybe all the great quarterbacks drink scotch. That's all I ever drank from the time I was young.

I drink it any way I can get it . . . with ice, without ice, with water, with soda. It doesn't make any difference. I'll even drink it right out of the bottle as long as it's scotch. After dinner Pete and I got in the sauce pretty good. We went out and partied and had a helluva time. We danced and raised hell and hollered and shouted and had a good time. Hell, we had just beat the world champs.

I don't mind if people bother me when I'm out after a game. Even when I'm eating, I'll still sign autographs. That's part of being an athlete. You have to expect it when you're a starting quarterback. You're a professional player and after you've been around a few years, people recognize you when you go out to a restaurant or a bar. I'll tell you. If you go out and don't get recognized, you get a little offended. At least I do.

That's part of the reason for playing football—the recognition you get. I think some players get a little irritated when they get asked for their autograph but they get even more irritated if people don't ask. Some athletes will give you this stuff about getting bothered and bugged by fans. I think a lot of that is bullshit. Everyone enjoys recognition.

I really think players enjoy it. They have to enjoy it or they wouldn't be in the game. It's part of our job when we are so-called celebrities. You're supposed to be asked for your autograph and be courteous to people.

The only hideaway I have is home. When I go out, I'm not trying to hide. I'm not going to go to a place where no one will recognize me. If I do go to a place where I don't want to be recognized, and then someone does, it screws up my whole night.

I'll say this: I wanted to be out and be recognized after we beat Pittsburgh.

9

The Knee

In the back of the mind of every professional football player is the fear of injury. And the most fearful of all injuries is to the knee. It can end a season or a career for a player. For Ken Stabler that fear became reality when he was injured in the second game of the season, a victory over the Kansas City Chiefs on September 20.

I was aware that the guy who hit me was a linebacker . . . the middle linebacker, Jimbo Elrod. I knew that the linebackers were coming. First thing I thought of was it's man-to-man coverage and I have someone to throw to. All I have to do now is find him.

Then I got hit. Right at the time I wasn't aware of exactly who it was who hit me. I watched the films because I wanted to find out how it happened and if it was a late hit. It wasn't a cheap shot.

He didn't know I had already thrown the ball. Someone bumped him. He was falling a little bit and he couldn't help it. It was one of those freak things and that's the way most injuries happen.

That's how it is. Someone falls into your leg. It hardly ever happens that you get hurt on a clean tackle. Someone gets blocked into you. I got it that way a couple years ago against Cleveland. Gene Upshaw was blocking Jerry Sherk and he blocked him right into me. He fell on my leg. There's nothing that can be done about something like that. The linemen are blocking and things happen.

I hold the ball a long time, which means the guys have to block longer and the defensive linemen are going to be closer to me. Maybe every one of the receivers is covered or you have trouble reading the coverage.

There's an unwritten law that the defensive people don't hit the quarterback below the knees. I've seen lots of times when defensive linemen could have taken shots at my knees but they didn't. That's one of the good things about pro football. Nobody really wants to hurt anyone else intentionally.

They could hit you low if they really wanted to. The first thing they are taught is to get their hands up so they can block a pass or at least obstruct your vision. They always wind up slapping you on the side of the head, hitting you around the shoulders, or clubbing you down to the ground. Hardly ever do they dive into your legs.

I don't think anyone would do it to me even if he had the chance. If there is a guy who cheap-shots a quarterback, the word gets around and eventually someone will get him. If someone doesn't follow the unwritten rules, he'll get it sooner or later.

There are other players in the league who players on our team think are cheap-shot artists and they'll do little things to get back at them.

I don't think there is any bounty on quarterbacks. You used to hear stories about teams putting up money that went to a player who got the quarterback on the other team and put him out of the game. I know it doesn't happen on our team and I haven't heard of any team in football doing it now. I think if you concentrate too much on getting the quarterback you have to neglect other parts of the game.

My first thought when I get hurt is how serious it is. That's the first thought I guess that would go through anyone's mind. It can knock you out for the year or even for a career.

After I finish thinking about how bad it is, I ask myself if I can continue to play. What's the next play? Can I get things going again?

I knew this injury wasn't as serious as some that happened to me earlier in my career. I've had two knee operations and I know what it takes to get hurt that bad. This was serious enough so that I couldn't play anymore. I didn't want to take a chance of it getting any worse. I knew it was enough to finish me for the day. It was the ligaments. Strained or stretched. I'm really not sure.

It's really sore when it first happens. And then it gets kind of numb. Then after that it gets weak. You can't put any pressure on it. It hurts to walk. It will be weak and sore for a while but then you can feel it start to get better again.

I gave some thought to going back in to play. Maybe I could have. I could have strapped it up and played. But there wasn't really any need. The score was 24–7 when I got hurt and we had the game under control. If the score had been tied, or we had been three points or seven down, I wouldn't have hesitated to go back into the game. I've played hurt before. I can cope with pain but I didn't see any reason for it when we're ahead and have the game under control.

I've played with worse injuries than this one. Sometimes you just have to do it.

When Kansas City started scoring I thought about going back in. But by then the knee was stiff and sore because I had been out for a while. If you are going back in, you're better off going right back in after you get hurt. Then it doesn't have a chance to stiffen up. The longer you sit, the stiffer it gets.

It wasn't until Tuesday that I realized I might not be able to play against Houston in this week's game. I wanted to play and felt I could have played. But it was John Madden's decision that I wouldn't play.

I remember what happened in 1975. I got hurt in the first half against San Diego. Then I went back in and played in the second half when I shouldn't have. My knee wasn't right and I struggled for several games after that. I threw a lot of interceptions. I don't alibi for anything but two-thirds of those interceptions were because of my leg.

Hell, I couldn't move around. I couldn't zip the ball. I couldn't put any pressure on my leg. I threw the ball early sometimes because I was afraid someone might hit my leg and really put me out. I hurt the team because I tried to play with my knee hurt. John Madden didn't want that to happen again this year.

After taking the week off I really felt good. I know Coach Madden was thinking about losing me for one game instead of taking a chance on losing me for the whole season.

One thing that makes a player valuable is how durable he is. That's important to me, to be able to play and have the team count on me. Coach Madden told me at the quarterback meeting the night before the game that I wasn't going to play. I don't know if he told Mike Rae he was going to start. Mike says no one ever did tell him he was going to start until the game. But I'm sure he knew. At the quarterback meeting a lot of the questions were directed to him.

After the meeting was over, John told me he didn't care if we lost, even if it was 50–0; it was his decision and he was going to live with it. He made the right decision because we won the game.

I just don't like sitting on the bench. I did it for three or four years and it was the worst part of my career. It's awful.

Watching that game in Houston from the sidelines wasn't any fun either. I talked to Mike several times during the game. When he came out he would ask me what I thought about certain plays. I made some suggestions but I didn't try to bug him or call the game for him. I didn't try to tell him a lot of things.

I knew what he faced. When the quarterback comes off the field, five different people hit you. The guys on the phones upstairs want to talk to you. Coach Madden wants to talk to you. The offensive line coach wants to tell you about some running play he thinks will work. And then Tom Flores, the quarterback coach, is on the phone with something about some pass plays.

Madden wants to talk about things in general. Then the wide receivers—Cliff Branch and Fred Biletnikoff—will come over and tell you some things they think they can do.

I helped him with some things that he asked me about and I made some suggestions but he really didn't need that much help. He did a good job.

We had talked just before the game. He asked me what he should call on the first play of the game. I told him it depended on where we got the ball. If we got a good run back to their 30-yard line, I told him I would throw a pass from there. But if it was just a normal runback, to about our 30-yard line, I would call a running play so everyone can just fire out, get hit, and get the butterflies out—something with straight-ahead blocking with the fullback carrying.

But Mike wanted me to give him a play to call. I told him: "East Far Right, 69, U Lead Man." It's a play we have with the fullback carrying. That's what he called. It gained about four yards but it got everyone firing out. That's what it's designed to do. After that, everything was cool.

It was Mike's game thereafter. John Madden called some plays for him and Tom Flores upstairs on the phone called some. Everything went very well—well enough for us to win, 14–13.

During the game, on the sidelines, I talked to Fred Biletnikoff a lot. We talked about the Astrodome—what an unusual stadium it is. We talked some football and sometimes we just shot the breeze. We talked about the coverages they were using on pass plays. And we talked about their players. Then we got talking about what time our plane would get back to Oakland that night.

When Mike Rae got sacked, I thought about me being in there and getting hit. And then I saw how well Mike was moving around. He kept from getting sacked a couple times and I knew if I had been in there I wouldn't have been able to do that with a bad knee. I would have either had to eat the ball or just fall down. Houston is a good team. They're going to get their share of sacks no matter who they play against.

I watched our offensive line to see how they handled some situations. When I'm playing I want to know what went wrong if our line breaks down. If our left tackle, Art Shell, is having trouble with a good defensive end like Cedrick Hardman of the 49ers, then I'm going to keep one of the backs in close to help out on the blocking.

If John Vella, the other tackle, is having trouble with someone like Jack Youngblood of the Rams, I'll keep a back in to give him help on that side. I want to know who's having trouble so I can help him.

For that reason, in a game like Houston, I watch and file things away. If I see Curley Culp of Houston giving our center, Dave Dalby, trouble, I'll file that away. Then the next time we play them, I'll make sure I have someone to help Dave. But he handled Curley very well and didn't need help.

When the game got close, I thought there might be some chance I would go in and play. But John Madden stuck by his decision. As long as I wasn't going to play, I wondered why I should even be in uniform. I guess it was for psychological reasons. If our players saw that I wasn't in uniform, they might think I was hurt worse than I really was.

And it can work on Houston too. If they see me over there on the sidelines in uniform, they have to be wondering if I will play. It's just something else for them to think about.

I didn't enjoy watching the game. It really eats at

me not being able to play even when I know I shouldn't be playing. I hate to stand there and watch other people do things when I want to be doing them. I want to be a part of it . . . the hoopla and then the stuff in the locker room afterward.

After the game I just got dressed and got on the bus. I was happy we won but I didn't have anything else to be happy about because I wasn't a part of it. I felt out of it.

My knee feels fine now. Not 100 percent. It's never going to be perfect because I've had two operations. I don't think it's so serious now that I'll need another operation but over the years it could. That's what happened to my other knee. I just kept getting it bumped around and pieces were breaking off. When they break off they grow. There were four or five pieces in there—about the size of the eraser on a pencil. They had to go in there and clean all that crap out. Those pieces can get in the joint and it locks up.

When I'm not playing, I don't like to pick up the newspaper on Monday morning and read about Bert Jones throwing two touchdown passes or Terry Bradshaw or Steve Grogan doing something good. I don't like to read about other quarterbacks doing things when I'm not doing it too. I'm competitive in that way. I want to do better than they do. And I want to win.

I don't make a big thing about it but I know what every other quarterback in the league does every week. I know how many touchdowns they threw and how many interceptions they had. I'm sure they probably do the same thing.

But it isn't how I'm playing that counts. If I'm playing good and we're winning, that's cool. Or if I'm not playing so good but we're winning, that's still all right. If I'm playing super and we're losing, or not putting points on the board, something is wrong. If you have great stats and you lose, you didn't get your job done.

This week we play New England. When the schedule first came out, everyone figured that game was a breather for us. Now they've won two games in a row, over Pittsburgh and Miami. They're playing good football. People don't realize there aren't any breathers on the schedule anymore.

Our division was supposed to be easy. But then San Diego hammers the hell out of St. Louis, a damn good team. They scored 43 points. Dan Fouts had a great day. He'll be leading the league in passing.

New England will really be riding high against us. We play them back there. They're making the big plays. That's how they are winning. We have to keep them from making the big plays or they could beat us. I really believe that.

10

Lesson in New England

After opening the 1976 season with a dramatic 31–28 comeback victory over the world champion Pittsburgh Steelers and then beating the Kansas City Chiefs and Houston Oilers, the Raiders had to expect a letdown. They got it on October 3 against the New England Patriots at Foxboro, Massachusetts.

There are some games you lose that you can't really get upset about because there is nothing you can do about it. Everything New England did was right and everything we did was wrong and it was that way from the very start of the game.

New England is a very good team. They're 100 percent better than the last time we played them because they have a new coach and a lot of new players. We knew they were improved. Hell, they beat Pittsburgh and Miami the two weeks before we played them. We saw movies of those games and the Patriots won because they were the better team. There wasn't anything lucky about it.

We were using a new defense, a 3–4 with an extra linebacker. We had so many of our regular defensive linemen hurt that we had to go to something different and it was using the extra linebacker. It isn't anything new in football but it was new to us. New England uses the same defense and Miami has used it.

They took advantage of our people on the inside. They have big running backs. That Sam Cunningham must weigh about 240 and their guards are even bigger. They concentrated on running up the middle. That meant that our guy in the middle had to take on their center, maybe a guard double-teaming him and then the running back. He didn't have much chance.

The Patriots didn't get fancy. They just kept running that same play until we bunched our defenses in the middle and then they would throw the ball. It was a smart game plan. It took advantage of our defense because we were not familiar with what we were doing. We didn't do anything right on either offense or defense but you have to give New England credit for some of that.

Fumbles hurt us. The first time we had the ball we had a little drive going and Clarence Davis lost the ball. Steve Zabel recovered for them. He seemed to be everywhere. They scored in about six plays by just running the ball. Andy Johnson took it over from the two. Then we got the ball again and had a good drive going. We had to throw the ball because our running game wasn't going too well. We got down to about the 12-yard line but then Mark van Eeghen fumbled. That's the kind of day it was. Mark doesn't fumble very often. Zabel was there to get the ball for the Patriots. They went the length of the field to score on a 21-yard pass from Steve Grogan to Darryl Stingley, making it 14–0.

If we had scored it would have been 7–7. We weren't worried after they went ahead, 14–0. We know we can score and score quickly. We were still in the game. There wasn't any letdown in the huddle. Everybody thought we were going to win. We got another drive going the next time we had the ball. We got down to their 20-yard line but then I got sacked for a loss. We were too far away to kick a field goal so we punted.

That was another turning point. We had a chance to tie the game and we didn't do it. We didn't get any more chances after that. It really got frustrating in the third quarter. They were ahead, 28–10, after they scored the first time they had the ball. But that's nothing in pro football. We scored 17 points in four minutes against the Steelers in the first game of the season and the Steelers are a helluva lot better than the Patriots.

The next time we had the ball we got a good drive going. We got down to their 6-yard line and I threw a touchdown pass to Dave Casper, our tight end. But Fred Biletnikoff got called for offensive interference and the touchdown was called back. That put us back on the 16-yard line. I called another pass only to Casper because New England wasn't covering him that close. I figured they wouldn't be looking for another pass to Casper after the last one was called back.

We scored again but this time Gene Upshaw was called for holding and that one didn't count either. Then on the next play I fumbled the ball when Tony McGee hit me and they recovered. That was the point of no return because they went right down and scored again to make it 35–10. If we had gotten either of the touchdowns that were called back, it would have been 28–17 with a whole quarter to play and we would have had a chance.

It's tough when you get behind early in the game and have to play catch-up. I didn't want to throw the ball as much as I did but I had to. They were letting us throw to Casper so I kept doing it. But that was smart on their part. They didn't let us complete any long passes to Fred Biletnikoff and Cliff Branch. Biletnikoff only caught one pass and Cliff didn't get any.

We had our chances but we screwed them up. It was just a bad day all around. Our defense saved us against Houston but this time they put the offense in the position of having to score every time we had the ball. Even if we had scored every time, it still might not have been enough. We were playing a very hot team.

I wasn't surprised when Coach Madden took me out of the game in the fourth quarter. We had to start thinking about the next game. There wasn't any way we were going to beat New England so there was no sense taking a chance of getting some key players hurt in a lost cause. They ended up with a 48–17 victory.

It taught us a lesson. You have to be ready to play

hard every week. You can't look at another team and figure you can beat them without giving your best effort. We took the Patriots lightly. I don't think we will if we play them again.

University of Alabama

That's me at Alabama. When I was growing up, every kid in Alabama wanted to play for Bear Bryant.

Below, I'm looking for a receiver in the Sugar Bowl against Nebraska. We beat them and I ended up as MVP.

UPI

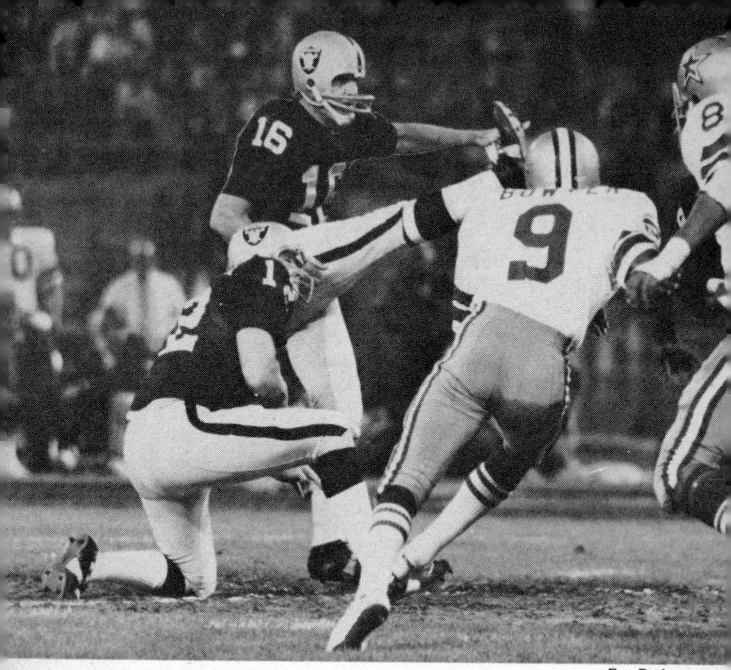

Ray DeAragon

Ken Stabler Collection

Above, it seemed like every time we needed a miracle to win a game, there was George Blanda doing it. I held the ball for him for seven years. This was against Dallas in 1974.

This was in a celebrity tournament in Montgomery, Alabama. I shoot high 80s, low 90s.

There were only 26 seconds remaining when I threw this pass to Clarence Davis in the end zone to give us a 28-26 victory over Miami in the 1974 AFC playoffs.

UPI

Below, L.C. Greenwood knocked me down here in our losing playoff against the Steelers in 1974.

Ray DeAragon

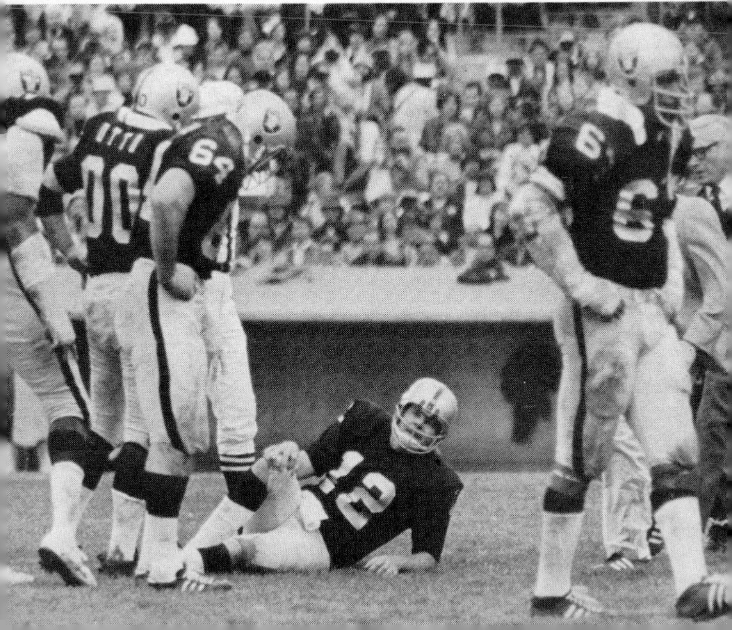

Joe Melena

Oakland Raiders

Above left, I'm feeling bad, and with good reason. I've just been intercepted in the Pittsburgh playoff game. That's our center, Joe Dalby, alongside me. What I like about Al Davis (above right) is his dedication to making us the Super Bowl champions. Below, John Madden is not your average coach. He lets us go and gives us a free wheel. I really enjoy watching him on the sidelines when I'm not playing. He stomps around like a big bear. But let me say that I think he should get more credit than he does.

Ray DeAragon

This is the Raider offense: Clarence Davis (28), Cliff Branch (21), Art Shell (78), Gene Upshaw (63), Dave Dalby (50), George Buehler (64), John Vella (75), Fred Biletnikoff (25), Mark van Eeghan (30), Dave Casper (87). Don't forget me (12).

Oakland Raiders

Ray DeAragon

This was at our Monday TV game against Cincinnati. I was 16-for-20 that night.

Below, I'm getting good protection in the Super Bowl.

UPI

Ray DeAragon

Above, the only time I really got hit in the Super Bowl was when Alan Page (88) sacked me.

UPI

John Madden is riding high after we won it all.

UPI

UPI

Above, Tony Dorsett of the University of Pittsburgh has the Maxwell trophy and I've got the Bert Bell trophy. The awards won't mean a thing when we play against each other.

I can't wear it when I'm playing, but I'm proud of being winner of the Hickok "Professional Athlete of the Year" belt. It's diamond-studded and gold-buckled.

11

Back on the Track

The Raiders had little time to lick their wounds after the humiliation in Foxboro. They had to play two good teams on the road—the Chargers at San Diego on October 10 and the Broncos in Denver on October 17. Ken Stabler knew his work was cut out for him.

I think maybe what happened in New England woke us all up. We thought we could just go out on the field and win because we were the Oakland Raiders.

Hell, there aren't any easy teams in the NFL. We found out that the Patriots were a damn good team. We had to get things going again. And we had to do it on the road—against San Diego and Denver.

We were tied for the AFC West lead at 3–1 with San Diego and Denver when we met the Chargers. So there was the lead at stake and I'm sure a lot of people were wondering how we'd bounce back.

We had a lot of injuries on defense—going into the game—but we didn't snap. We gave up 17 points. I had a good day passing and Cliff Branch and Dave Casper had the same catching. I had great protection, completing 20 of 26 for 339 yards and three touchdowns. Branch kept the Charger secondary confused; he caught five passes for 167 yards and two touchdowns. Casper caught seven for 104 yards. And we won, 27–17.

I've got to say we've got a great offensive line. We go for the deep patterns so our line has to block a little longer than the other teams. There's always that bullshit from the opposition that our linemen hold. Why don't they just give them credit for doing a good job?

Tommy Prothro, the San Diego coach, was complaining about the holding. Do you think he would have said anything if his team had won? You're damn right he wouldn't.

We had trouble with our running game at the start of the season because Marv Hubbard was hurt. But now it's starting to get going. We just don't know how it's going to be in any game. We might pass for 300 yards and run for 50. Or it might be 250 on the ground and I'll throw for only 100.

It really doesn't matter. The only thing we care about is winning. They never ask how you did it.

I see the statistics on a team that has given up a lot of yards on passes and you would think we would plan on passing against them. You can't always do that. I can't just say, "I should have a good day passing against them." There are quite a few reasons why a team might be giving up yards passing and you have to know the right one.

We play our games one play at a time. I know that sounds corny but we do. We do what the defense dictates. Maybe the other teams stack their defense to stop our passing. It would be silly to throw against a situation like that. That's when you run the ball. It can depend on the down and distance. If it's second and 10 or third and 8, you have a tendency to throw the ball. But it doesn't mean you have to.

That was the way it was in our next game against Denver. We ran the ball and gained 20 yards. Then we ran the ball again and made nine yards. With second and one, we ran the ball again. I know there are some quarterbacks who think you have to throw in that situation. But maybe that's what the defense is expecting so you go for the first down instead.

I always try to put myself in the position of the middle linebacker on the other team. I ask myself what play he would be looking for in the situation. Then I try to do something else. You can't always do that but it's a good way some of the time.

If you get a running game going, you stick with it. That's just basic football. Afterward, someone might ask, "How come you didn't throw the ball more?" Hell, what difference does it make as long as you win?

John Madden feels the same way. When we have our quarterback meeting before each game, he goes over the game plan. He always says the same thing. "There is a way to win every game. All you have to do is find it."

Once we get the game plan, we stick to it as close as possible. But then the situation changes as the game goes on. If you get behind, you might have to throw the ball more even if that wasn't part of the game plan. If you get a lead, you don't throw the ball. That's the way it has to be. That's why you can't make up your mind before the game starts.

We always have some special things we want to do. The coaches remind us to look for special situations, defenses that the other team gets into that we can take advantage of. Or it might be a player. We'll watch a defensive back in the first half and see how he reacts to certain things. Then in the second half we might take advantage of his tendencies.

Every defense has some weaknesses. The quarterback has to find them or the assistant coaches upstairs have to do it. When I see the defense ganged up in one spot, I know there has to be a weakness somewhere else. But that doesn't mean you make a change at the line of scrimmage. I've never been too crazy about calling audibles at the line of scrimmage.

Too many things can go wrong. The other 10 players have to hear what you say and then think about the change in a split second. It's also hard for the wide receivers to hear sometimes because of the noise. The time I will do it is when I call a play and then get to the line of scrimmage and see a defense I don't like. Then I just say: "Oh, oh. I better call something else" and I do with an audible.

I go over plays in my mind. Several days before the game I'm thinking of situations that might come up and what I would call. When I'm on the sidelines during the game, I'll talk with the coach and also the other quarterbacks to see if they noticed anything that might help. Sometimes it's just a little thing but that can win a game with one big play.

It was like that in the Denver game when Cliff Branch told me he could beat his man on an "up" pattern. I called the play and he beat his man. That was a big play in helping us win the game, 17–10.

There are other times when we really don't care what defense the other team is in. We figure our players are better than theirs and we'll beat them at their strong point. That can demoralize them. Football isn't just offense against defense either. The special teams can make a big difference. We beat Denver with our special teams.

Morris Bradshaw did a good job of containing Rick Upchurch, the best punt-return man in the league. Except for the great catch that Cliff Branch made, the offense was mediocre. We scored enough points to win but that's about all you can say about it.

We were really inconsistent and struggling in the first half. But we can't be too critical of ourselves. Hell, you have to give some credit to the other team and Denver has a great defense. We had a good drive going in the first quarter but then I threw an interception. It was a stupid interception because there were two defensive guys right where I threw the ball.

I never should have thrown the ball. That was my fault. That had nothing to do with how good the team we were playing was. It was just plain stupid on my part.

The next time we got the ball I got sacked and we never recovered and had to punt. The third time we had the ball I tried to surprise them by throwing the ball on first down. But our left tackle, John Vella, got beat by his man and I lost 10 yards on the play. That's what I meant about trying to do something different. Sometimes the other team anticipates what you are going to do. It wasn't Vella's fault that he got beat and I was sacked. That's to the credit of the defensive man who got me.

John Madden never says anything to me after an interception even if I make a stupid throw. He knows I know it was bad and he doesn't have to tell me. I'm not playing that bad so far this year. I've had eight interceptions in six games. I've thrown the ball about 150 or 160 times.

If I were throwing a lot of interceptions and not many touchdown passes, I would expect Madden to get on me about it. I've thrown for 11 touchdowns in six games. Madden knows that him telling me about one stupid interception isn't going to help anyone concerned. The point is I know when I've made a dumb throw.

12

The Green Bay Experience

Penalties, like fumbles and interceptions, can be frustrating for a quarterback. The height of frustration for Ken Stabler during the 1976 season came on October 24 against the Green Bay Packers, when Oakland was called for 13 penalties that cost 119 yards. In one stretch of 11 plays in the third quarter, there were seven penalties called—four on Oakland and three on Green Bay. The game had significance for Stabler on another count: it was the first time he'd played against a Green Bay team.

We expect to have some trouble with the Green Bay pass defense. They've got Willie Buchanon back there and he's good. He's slowed down a little from a couple years ago because he had a broken leg . . . in fact I think he broke the same leg twice.

They have good defensive backs and he's the best of them. The people who have thrown the ball against him so far this season haven't done much. I've watched them on films. But it's hard for me to evaluate a defensive back unless I have actually played against him. I have to see what he'll do against Fred Biletnikoff or Cliff Branch. Then I can judge better.

I've never played against Green Bay before. I was with the Raiders when they played them back there in 1972. Daryle Lamonica was the quarterback. We won the game and I didn't get in.

Playing the Packers is like playing the New York Yankees in baseball. They have all that tradition but it isn't so much like that anymore. That was when Vince Lombardi was the coach. He won all the championships for them. Him and Paul Hornung and Jim Taylor and Bart Starr. You still remember all those guys. How could you forget them? Max McGee and Jerry Kramer. When I was young, the Green Bay Packers were THE team in pro football.

Bart Starr. What a quarterback he was! He was from Alabama too. I met him once when I was younger. He had a Mercury distributorship in Alabama and I went by and met him. I've talked to him a couple times since then. I enjoy talking to other quarterbacks. When he was a senior at Alabama, the team went 0–10. They didn't win a game.

He was drafted in the 17th round by Green Bay and that's about as low as you can be. But that didn't bother him. He went on to be all-pro and win a couple Super Bowls for them. You've got to really hand it to him for what he's done and is continuing to do. He winds up as the coach of the Packers and I consider it a pleasure just to play against a team coached by anyone as great as he was.

He's turned things around a little since he took over. They struggled over the years after Lombardi left. But now things are going better. Eventually, Bart will get his people in there playing for him. Hell, they're not a bad team right now. They have some very good people. Like Mike McCoy. He's a tough one. And Fred Carr, a great linebacker. Then there's Willie Buchanon in the secondary.

The only player I know on their team is Gary Weaver, one of the linebackers. He used to play for us. I know he's good and I'm not surprised he leads them in tackles. He's playing as well as anyone from what I saw on film.

They've only given up four touchdown passes in six games. That's really something. I'm looking forward to playing them.

In one of their more inconsistent performances, the Raiders whipped the Packers, 18–14. Stabler completed 13 of 21 passes for 220 yards and three touchdowns. All three scoring passes came in the second quarter when Oakland scored all its points. It was a mediocre performance for Stabler.

It wasn't pretty but we won. We made the big plays when we had to make them. The referees controlled the game. Penalties can even things up between two teams. There was no question in my mind that we were a better team than the Packers, much better than the score indicates.

It seemed like every time we would get something going there would be a holding penalty. We were in the hole and had a hard time getting out. The same thing happened to the Packers. There were 13 penalties on us and 13 on them. That doesn't give you much chance to play football.

We won because we have great receivers. The other team can't cover them all. If I have time to look, I'll find one of them open. If they're open, they will catch the ball. Cliff Branch made a great catch on his touchdown and so did Fred Biletnikoff.

Green Bay played good defense just like we expected. But that didn't decide the game. It was the penalties. I don't think anyone likes to see so many. I believe the officials are trying to prove something. I think they want the fans to be aware they are on the field.

They seem to be saying, "See, I can throw my flag and call a play back." I think they are doing it purposely and it's really hurting football. They may think they're righting a wrong by calling so many penalties but they seem to forget that the fans come to see two teams play football, not to watch them drop their hankies all over the field.

I've never played in a football game where I was more frustrated than against Green Bay. I try not to let things like penalties and interceptions bother me but I'll have to admit this really got to me. The officials took all the fun out of it. I don't mind having the other team take the fun out of the game by knocking me down. That's part of the game and I expect it.

But all those damn penalties don't add a thing. It's hard for me to accept the fact that there are two teams out on the field playing their asses off trying to win and then some guy throws a flag and destroys everything you're trying to do. I'm not saying there shouldn't be officials. Hell, if we didn't have them we would probably kill each other out there. All I can say is I'm happy that we beat Green Bay.

The penalties ruined our continuity whenever we seemed to get anything going. You had to change your thinking all the time. We would run a play that would gain 15 yards and I'd be thinking what I was going to call on the next play—based on the down and the distance. Then I would see a flag thrown and instead of a first down, it would be second and 20 yards to go. It got so bad I was losing interest in the game. I came very close to going over to the referee and asking: "What are you guys trying to do?"

It didn't make any sense to me. It wasn't just in our game that the penalties were being called. It was happening all over the league. They called more than 50 penalties in a game between Seattle and Tampa Bay. As I understand it, there wasn't any special directive from the NFL office to tell the officials to call more penalties. They just started calling them.

Most of the penalties were for holding. I've never seen the kind of stuff they were calling guys for holding. I can understand it when they call penalties on a guy who does something violent, like rough up the quarterback or grab someone by the face mask. It's all the chickenshit stuff. I've heard they could call a holding penalty on every play if they really wanted and maybe that's their goal.

Don't get me wrong. There are some holding penalties that should be called and sometimes I'm happy to see one of our guys get called for holding. If he gets beat by his man, and he grabs the guy to keep him from hitting me, the penalty should be called. But when they call holding penalties on guys who are just blocking at the line of scrimmage, I don't think that's right.

The defensive man has all the advantages anyway. He can slap the blocker in the head. One time is legal but sometimes a guy will do it several times and he doesn't get called for it. I can't blame the blocker for getting mad and grabbing the defensive man if he keeps getting slapped around.

The penalties didn't just hurt us. They destroyed Green Bay too. I'm not bitching about it because we got called for a bunch of penalties. Hell, we won the game. We've got nothing to bitch about. I just don't think it's good for football.

Coach Madden told us after the game to try not to let the penalties bother us. He said it was sour grapes to complain about the officiating after you lose a game. Maybe that's why I'm doing it now as a winner.

It wouldn't be like Tommy Prothro, the San Diego coach, complaining about penalties after we beat them. He lost the game and that is sour grapes when he blames the officials.

Penalties slow down the game. The fans don't want to see a team having third down and 20 yards to go all the time. Then you have to throw the ball and the other team knows it.

What makes football so great is being able to do something the other team doesn't expect. All the holding penalties have a tendency to make the offensive linemen less aggressive. They won't block hard because they're afraid they'll get called for holding. Maybe that's why so many quarterbacks are getting hurt this season. I got hit more times in the Green Bay game than I have in a long time. In the third quarter, Gene Upshaw, one of our guards, told me he was afraid to move.

"They'll call a holding penalty on me," he said. As a result I'm getting the hell knocked out of me. That isn't right. You knock out all the top quarterbacks and that can't be good for football. Or us quarterbacks.

I would like to see something put in to protect the quarterbacks. I'm not saying I expect to play the game with a coat and tie on but there should be something to protect us from some guy who wants to get in a cheap shot.

We don't talk about it in the huddle. There's too many other things to do. But when we're on the sidelines we do. The linemen will tell me they didn't hold their man but they still get called for it. They weren't apologizing. There wasn't anything that can be done about it. After the game, we watch the films and we can look for the holding penalties that have been called. Sometimes we see them and sometimes we don't. Some of them are ridiculous.

There was really a bad one on George Buehler in the Green Bay game. Buehler never holds. He's so damn honest he wouldn't break a rule under any circumstances. We saw it in the films. He was blocking Mike McCoy, the big Packer tackle. He hit him in the stomach with his head, just drove right into him like a lineman is allowed to do. When McCoy got hit, he bent over and pinned Buehler's head against his stomach. The official called Buehler for holding. I don't see how they can possibly call something like that because it wasn't even close to holding.

There was another one they called on Clarence Davis, our running back, in the New England game. He was a pass receiver and was running a pattern. He wasn't even close to another player and he was called for holding. Who was he holding? I can't understand why or how an official would make a mistake like that. I guess no one is perfect.

In one of the Monday night TV games an official

called a piling-on penalty. They showed it on instant replay and it wasn't piling on. Anyone could see that. What made it even worse was that they had a microphone on the referee when he announced the penalty. He called it on the wrong player. The number wasn't right. That's inexcusable and I think a lot more of it goes on than we realize. Maybe it happened in other years too and we just weren't aware of it. Or maybe the officials now aren't as sharp as they used to be.

If you didn't have some rules or guidelines, it would be like the Watts riots. It would be a street fight and could really get nasty. I think there's a way to do it but throwing a penalty flag 25 or 30 times a game isn't it. One or two penalties at a crucial time in a drive is all it takes to get you beat in a game. We can look back after a game and see where one penalty at the wrong time killed a drive and maybe even lost the game.

How many times does a team miss the playoffs and a shot at the Super Bowl because of one loss? All that could be the result of one penalty at the wrong time. That's how much effect the officials can have. Penalties take all the entertainment out of football for the fans and can take money out of the pockets of the players.

I'll tell you how bad it was in the Green Bay game. Dave Casper, our tight end, got to feeling sorry for the Packers. That's not good. And John Vella, one of our tackles, was called for holding and two of the Green Bay players told him they knew he wasn't doing it.

I got to talking to their players during the game. It's something I do all the time. If a guy makes a nice play and tackles me, I tell him "nice play." That was the way it was with Alden Roche, the Packer defensive end. He's good and got me a couple times.

Another time Dave Roller of the Packers just missed getting me before I threw the ball. As he walked by me after the play he said: "I'm going to get you." It wasn't an angry thing. We both laughed about it. Later in the game I completed a pass and I asked him how he liked that.

Another time Roche was called for roughing me. It was a late hit and he knew it but he wasn't trying to hurt me. He didn't say he was sorry but I could tell he wasn't trying to knock me out of the game. There are some linemen who aren't that way. Some of them knock you down and then stand over you and call you names.

They'll say, "How do you like that, you son of a bitch?" I never say anything back to them. It just shows there are some class guys who play pro football and some who don't have any class.

You remember the ones who have class.

I've never gotten mad enough to go for anyone who knocked me down in a football game. I'm not a very emotional person. Quarterbacks can't afford to be emotional.

I'm too important to our team to take the chance of getting kicked out of the game because I go after someone. If I get thrown out, I'm letting down 40 other players. That's why I have to control my emotions. Of course, if I did decide to take a poke at someone it wouldn't matter how big he was. I'd do it.

But that's where emotions come into it. I can't be thinking about poking someone because then my mind isn't on football. I have to concentrate on calling plays. If someone gives me a bad time, we've got players on our team who will take care of the situation. John Vella is a pretty good cop.

If I took a poke at someone and broke my left hand, I could screw up my whole career. And I could screw up a whole season for a lot of other people. That's why I don't do it.

A quarterback has to play the game without emotion no matter what happens. He can be frustrated like I was with all the penalties in the Green Bay game. But you just have to forget it and keep on playing and doing your best.

Bart Starr was asked for his opinion of Stabler following the game. "He's a remarkable passer. He's great to watch even when he's chewing your team into little pieces," he said.

13

Knocked Goofy

After the Raiders put down Denver again, 19–6, on October 31 they played one of their most dramatic games–against the Bears on November 7 at Soldier Field in Chicago. Ken Stabler played a large part in the 28–27 victory, but his teammates had to tell him about it afterward. In the third quarter, Stabler was sacked by Chicago linebacker Don Rives. He was helped off the field and spent the remainder of the afternoon in a daze.

We knew the Chicago Bears would be tough. We watched them in films. They have an aggressive defensive line that really goes after the quarterback. We didn't think they could beat us but we expected a tough game. We made it tougher than it should have been with mistakes–fumbles and interceptions.

I guess the Bears thought they should have won it. They had a touchdown called back and the official admitted afterward that he made a mistake. But, hell, if the whistle hadn't blown, there was no way their big lineman would have run all the way to score.

It was one of those games where strange things just seem to happen. The wind was blowing to beat hell. I hear it usually does in Chicago. That was a big factor in the game. We got a 21–7 lead at the half and were moving the ball very well against them. Then all of a sudden they started to come back. Bam, they had a touchdown. And then, bam, they had another one. Just like that.

You learn in pro football that it's hard to get a safe lead. A team can come back so quickly that it's tough to ever think you have a safe lead. After they made the first score, we had a hard time moving the ball. We had the wind against us. They got a good punt and we had the ball inside our five-yard line. We couldn't do anything and they scored to make it 21–20.

Then, the next time they downed the ball inside our 10-yard line and we couldn't move again. We didn't get a good punt and they came right back and scored again to go ahead 27–21.

You've got to give the Bears credit. Their defense played very well. They're not as good as Denver as a unit but they can hit damn hard.

I can testify to that.

I'm really not sure what happened when I got hit. I went back to pass and the next thing I knew I was on the ground. I don't know who hit me. All I remember was getting hit in the back of the head and then hitting that hard artificial turf.

My legs went numb. I couldn't remember where I

was. Hell, I wasn't even sure who I was. That's the closest I've ever come to being completely knocked out in a football game. There were a couple times I had come close.

One time, Jack Youngblood of the Los Angeles Rams got me the same way. I never knew what hit me and was out of it for awhile. It's a funny feeling. I didn't know what was going on. I could hear the crowd cheering but I didn't know where I was.

Your natural instinct is to try to get up after you get knocked down. I hurt all over. My head hurt. My legs hurt and my whole body ached. It's hard to explain unless you've had it happen to you. The first thing I remember was everyone standing around me when I was on the ground. I guess that was after I tried to get up.

They helped me off the field. They just kind of dragged me. One of our trainers had me by each arm and they carried me off. Afterward, I thought I had walked off the field by myself. That's how fuzzy my head was. Once I got to the sidelines, I looked up at the clock. There were 10 minutes left but I didn't know what quarter it was. I asked David Humm and he said there were 10 minutes left to play in the game. I had no idea what had happened from the time I got hit until I asked him about the time. I don't know how long that was.

I was goofy as a pet coon.

I knew I was going to have to go back into the game and I stood there on the sidelines trying to clear my head. I had some smelling salts and some oxygen and that cleared it up a little. But I was still foggy. It was like I was somewhere else. My head never did get completely clear for the rest of the game.

Tom Flores, one of our assistant coaches, talked to

me on the telephone from the press box where he was helping call the plays. But when we were through talking, I realized I hadn't heard a word he said. At least, I couldn't remember anything he told me. I knew I hadn't heard him because when I did go back in the game, I didn't do anything he had told me to do.

When I did go back in, about three minutes after I got hurt, I fumbled the ball on the very first play. Wally Chambers, one of the Bear tackles, hit me as I was going back to pass. I dropped the ball and their defensive end, Roger Stilwell, picked it up and started to run for a touchdown. The referee, Chuck Heberling, said that he blew his whistle by mistake.

I heard the whistle and thought he meant it was an incomplete pass. I could have gone after Stilwell. So could John Vella or Art Shell. They were close enough to catch him but they didn't try because they heard the whistle. I just kind of stood there while they argued. It gave me some more time to clear my head. I kept shaking it to get it clear.

The referee admitted he made a mistake but he wouldn't give Chicago the touchdown. He did rule that I had fumbled the ball instead of calling it an incomplete pass. I didn't realize all this at the time. Somebody told me about it after the game.

Anyway, we didn't have the ball and that gave me some more time to recover. We were losing the game, 27–21, with about 10 minutes to play. We got the ball right back again when Ted Hendricks intercepted a pass and I went back in. I still had no idea what defense the Bears were using. I called running plays to give me more time to think. We made a few yards and then I had to throw a pass.

I called a play with Cliff Branch as the receiver but

when I got the ball from the center, I realized I had no idea where Branch was going to be. I threw the ball and it wasn't even close. Cliff might have been open and scored a touchdown but I never even saw him. It was like being in the middle of the trees and not realizing I was in a forest.

Hell, I might have called a play we didn't even have. But I didn't. I got the terminology right and I knew what plays I was calling. But then everything was fuzzy. I couldn't make out any individuals. Everything was like a blur. There was just a bunch of people running around and all that noise.

When I was in the huddle I was shaking my head. Gene Upshaw kept asking me if I was all right. He said I told him I was but I don't remember doing that either. The one thing I was aware of was the score of the game. I knew we had to get another touchdown or we were going to lose. After I overthrew Branch on the pass, we had to punt. Chicago had the ball for quite awhile and I had a chance to get my head clear.

We got the ball again with about five minutes to play and I knew it might be our last chance. I didn't give a damn what defense the Bears were in. I just started throwing the ball. I knew we had the wind behind us and that would help. I threw a pass for Fred Biletnikoff but it was broken up. I threw again and this time Clarence Davis caught it for a short gain. We had third down and had to get a first down. I threw to Cliff Branch and he caught it and ran to about midfield.

I was just taking a wild guess on what their defense was doing. I figured that Branch could outrun them no matter what the defense was. All I had to do was get the ball to him. We had the first down and Cliff told me he could beat his man deep. I called a pass play and threw the ball as far as I could. At least, I thought I threw the ball as far as I could. My depth perception must have been affected when I got hit in the head and the ball was short.

Cliff came back and tipped it up in the air. Then he caught it and went for the touchdown. Branch made a helluva play. He knocked the ball away from the defensive back and then caught it. I can't say I was surprised to see him catch the ball. He's done it before. When you put the ball in the air, anything can happen and this time it was good for us.

I can't remember what play it was I called. I can't remember anything about the first half of the game either. Later, on the plane, I could, but not at the end of the game. It's different when a quarterback gets hit in the head. He has to call the plays and there's a lot riding on what he says. I've seen other players who were almost knocked out. But they can still do their job. John Vella got kicked in the head in a game early in the season and I could tell he was almost out. But he still did his job. He blocked his man. I remember thinking how funny it was looking at him. It isn't funny after it happens to you. It hurts like hell.

After the touchdown play, I ran off the field and people came over to shake my hand and congratulate me. All I could think of was how lucky we were. I told Vella that. We still hadn't won the game. The pass to Branch tied the score and then Errol Mann kicked the extra point to put us ahead, 28–27.

There was four minutes to play and Chicago would get the ball at least one more time. They got a drive going and made a bunch of first downs. I was watching from the sidelines. By this time my head was pretty clear and I knew what was going on. I got to thinking I might have to go back in the game if they kicked a field goal. They got a first down on our 20-yard line and then ran a couple plays to use up time and get a little closer.

I was smelling an ammonia capsule when they lined up for the field goal on fourth down. I was trying to think what I would do if they made it. I figured we would have about 20 seconds . . . maybe time for one or two plays. The way the wind was blowing—and it was in our favor—I figured that if we did have to score again, I might be able to throw a couple of quick passes and get the ball up near midfield. Then Errol Mann might have a chance to make a 50-yard field goal. He was making them from 53 yards out in practice before the game.

While we were waiting for Chicago to try their field goal, Mann came over to me. "If we get to midfield, I'll make a field goal," he told me. I winked at him. I think both of us hoped we wouldn't have to try one.

Chicago played it smart. They let the clock run down as much as they could before they tried the field goal. They knew about the wind and didn't want to give us time to strike back. They knew we were capable of doing it. I guess they thought we were capable of just about anything after what we had done against Pittsburgh in the season opener.

I was watching when their kicker tried the field goal. There wasn't anything else to do. We just stood there on the sidelines and watched. When he first kicked it, I thought it was going to be good. It looked straight to me but then I thought maybe I'm not seeing things the way I should. But the wind caught it a little. It drifted to the right and hit the upright of the goalpost and bounced back.

All I could say was "I'm damn glad he missed."

Then I looked to see if there had been a penalty on the play. I didn't want him to get another chance from even closer. There was no penalty so I knew the game was over. There were 15 seconds left when I went back on the field. I took the snap from center and just lay down on the ground. That was it.

I'll tell you one thing when we play football. We always give the fans their eight bucks worth. One of our assistant coaches, Tom Dahms, didn't like it when someone said we were lucky to win. He said it wasn't luck; it takes a good team to win the close games. He's right. But we were lucky too.

We've been winning the close games all season long. We were struggling at the start of the year. We had quite a few injuries and our defense wasn't playing too well. They gave up a lot of points and that puts pressure on the offense to score more. We also had a lot of penalties and we overcame them. That's the mark of a good team too. We've managed to go 8–1 and that's a good sign. A lot of people were writing us off earlier in the season. Just like they did in the last two years. All the magazines pick us to win because they say we have so much talent. But then we don't win the big game so they say we choke. I think maybe that helped us this season. Some of the other teams may not be taking us as seriously as they should because we had so many injuries to key players.

I hope they keep doing it. Everyone thinks we're not very good because we haven't been killing our opponents. Maybe we can just slip in this year. We're going to make the playoffs. I know that. We're three games ahead with five to play. We're going to win our division and that puts us right where we've been for the past five years.

Maybe this is a year of destiny for us. It could be considering what happened in the Pittsburgh game and then in Houston and now against Chicago. Nothing that happens the rest of this season will surprise me after what we've gone through. It wouldn't surprise me if we do win the whole thing. I don't know if it's fate or luck or whatever. The football bounces funny and this season it's been bouncing our way.

Maybe the good bounces will come for us in the playoffs too. Hell, it would be about time. It seems like Pittsburgh always gets the good bounces in the playoffs. I don't care who we play in the playoffs. There was one wire story quoting one of the Pittsburgh players, Steve Furness. He said we didn't want to meet them in the playoffs. That's bullshit!

We don't care who we play. Once you get into the playoffs, the level of competition is so good it doesn't make any difference who you play. If a team isn't any good, it doesn't make the playoffs. You just have to go out there and try to beat whoever you play. We're capable of beating any team. We've already beat Pittsburgh, so why do they think we don't want to play them again?

What Furness said is a terrible thing for any professional athlete to say. He should know that anytime a professional athlete takes the field, he's going to bust his ass to win—particularly those who have been playing as long as some of us have.

You don't go out there and lie down. You go out there to try and win for your own self-pride. It doesn't matter what a win or a loss will do to your record or how it affects some other team.

Do you think I'm going to go out there and throw interceptions or incompletions? Do you think we're going to miss tackles on purpose? There's no way. We might use some nonstarters after we wrap up the title but that would be to protect some of our key players for the playoffs. That's just logic. But if we lose a game by doing it, guys like Furness are going to say we did it on purpose.

You're caught between a rock and a hard place. Pittsburgh wouldn't believe it no matter what we do. Aren't they aware of the home-field advantage that goes to the team with the best record in the conference? That can be a big thing in the championship game. Pittsburgh players should know that. We have to go 13–1 to have a chance of having the championship game at home. Even that wouldn't be good enough if Baltimore doesn't lose another game.

They could be 13–1 too. If they are, they would get the title game because their loss was outside their conference and ours was to New England, a team in the AFC. It's as simple as that. We have to win the rest of our games to get the championship game and hope Baltimore loses another game.

If that happens, maybe the Pittsburgh players will shut up.

14

Dumb Throws and Interceptions

The measure of quarterbacks in the NFL is the ability to complete passes for touchdowns and to avoid interceptions. And, of course, to win.

Ken Stabler has thrown his share of interceptions but has more than his share of touchdown passes. In a game against Kansas City at Oakland Coliseum November 14, Stabler saw four of his passes intercepted by the Chiefs. But he also threw two touchdown passes, and the Raiders won, 21–10.

If any quarterback says he doesn't mind having a pass intercepted, he's lying. It's the most frustrating thing that can happen. You get a good drive going and then throw an interception. You've wasted a lot of effort.

The quarterback who throws long passes has more of a chance of having interceptions than the guy who throws the safe, short passes. Throwing safe, short passes is not my idea of how to play football. If I miss on a long pass, I might come right back and throw another one. That's the Oakland Raiders' style of playing. We go for the big play as often as we can.

Interceptions are a part of the game. What you have to do is hold them down to a minimum. I don't care how good you think you are. They're going to happen. You can throw a perfect pass and it might bounce off the receiver's hands and get intercepted. There isn't anything you can do to prevent that. When you get a pass intercepted, you try to think what you could have done to prevent it. Sometimes there isn't anything. But if you don't read the coverage right or throw the ball poorly, there is something you can do.

You don't just write it off and forget it. The coaches upstairs will tell you what you did wrong because they can see from where they are. I want to know what the coverage was on an interception. I've made my share of dumb throws because I didn't recognize the coverage. After you figure out what you did wrong, you have to decide what effect the interception had on your team. If the other team scores a touchdown as a result of it, that's as bad as it can be.

But there are other times when an interception really doesn't hurt. Suppose you have third and 25 yards to go and you throw a 50-yard pass down to the other team's 10-yard line. What difference is it if it does get intercepted? If it was incomplete we would have had to punt on the next play anyway.

The one thing you can't do after an interception is let it bother you and change the way you play the game. You can't say that because you get a long pass intercepted, you won't throw long anymore. Tha would be stupid. You have to have enough confidence in yourself to complete the pass the next time. You also have to have confidence in your teammates to catch the ball.

For every interception you have, you should have at least one touchdown pass. That's one way to judge what kind of year a quarterback is having. You have to keep plugging after an interception. I always think positive. I figure I can throw the same pass that got intercepted for a touchdown if I throw it right.

Every time there is a pass intercepted, you have to analyze why it happened. The coaches are going to do it when they watch the films of the game. Sometimes you have to give the defensive team credit for making a good play. Hell, that's their job. There are some very good defensive backs who will make an interception sometimes no matter how well the quarterback throws the ball. It's different if you overthrow the receiver or don't throw the ball far enough. No one has to tell you that.

If you read the coverage wrong, you try to learn from it. You file away how the other team reacted on a certain pass play. Maybe you can do something to take advantage of it later in the game. Or the next time you play the team. That doesn't mean it won't happen again. Sometimes you think you've got a pass completed and a guy makes a diving interception. You throw the same pass and it happens again. The Pittsburgh defensive backs are good at that. Mike Wagner did that to me twice in a game. I saw him do something on the first interception and I thought I could take advantage of it the next time. But he intercepted the next one too. So much for smart-ass quarterbacks.

I've had passes intercepted every way they can be.

I don't think there is any other way I could do it. The whole point is that you try to avoid it but if you don't, you just keep throwing the ball and taking your chances. The four interceptions against Kansas City were the most I've ever had in a game. I've had four intercepted before but never more than that.

I don't think it ever happened in high school or college because I didn't throw the ball that much in those days. I did it in the first game this season but people seem to forget that. That was the Pittsburgh game. But I also threw three touchdown passes and we won, 31–28. That's all people remember is who won the game.

You can see that in the stories in the paper on Monday. It might say, "Ken Anderson threw three touchdown passes to lead the Cincinnati Bengals to a victory" or it might say, "The Chicago Bears picked off four of Fran Tarkenton's passes and beat the Vikings."

It's always a big deal for a quarterback on interceptions and touchdown passes. If you win, no one notices. The only way you can find out if a quarterback had a bad day and his team won is to look at the statistics. If I throw an interception and it costs us the game, I expect people to get on me. That's when it's my fault we lost. I had some interceptions in the game that we lost to New England early in the season. But it was no big deal. New England played so well they were going to win no matter what we did. We made it a little easier for them with all the fumbles, interceptions, and penalties.

The only time an interception is bad is when it costs you a game. Don't get me wrong. I don't like interceptions. I'm not happy about having 15 interceptions so far this season. But we have won 9 out of 10 games so I must be doing something right.

I have an article that some girl wrote for one of the papers. It says Ken Stabler threw two touchdown passes and the Raiders ran for 211 yards and beat the Kansas City Chiefs, 21–10. If we had lost the game, the story would have said Stabler had four interceptions and the Raiders were beaten, 21–10, by Kansas City. The bottom line is winning and it doesn't make any difference how you do it. If you have a quarterback who gets some passes intercepted but he's winning games for you, he's doing something right. There's no substitute for that.

The only time you really look at statistics is at the end of the season. The NFL has a complicated way of determining who the best quarterback is. It's based on the number of passes you throw, the number you complete, how many yards you gain, how many touchdown passes you have and how many interceptions. One quarterback might be the best in the league in completions and yards gained but still not be the top quarterback. He might not have many touchdown passes or quite a few interceptions.

If you have 20 touchdown passes and 10 interceptions I would say that's a good season as long as your team is winning. But 10 touchdown passes and 10 interceptions is not good. Right now I'm 20 and 15—20 touchdown passes and 15 interceptions. That's not bad. If it weren't for the 15 interceptions, I would be leading the league in passing. But the Raiders are leading the league so it doesn't matter to me. I've led the league in passing before. What I want to do is win the Super Bowl. I don't give a damn how many interceptions I have if I do that.

I am the number two passer even with all the interceptions. I'm not rattling off my statistics just to be impressive. The point is that even with 15 interceptions, I'm doing okay. It's like when you're running a business. You can do some things wrong but the president of the company looks at that bottom line. If it's in black ink, that's good. If it's red, that's bad. He doesn't really care why it's that way.

Right now the bottom line I want is 13–1 and winning the Super Bowl. I don't care how the hell we do it. And I don't think anyone else does either.

15

Conquering Eagles

There are some teams in the NFL that Ken Stabler knows almost as well as he does his own—the Kansas City Chiefs, the Denver Broncos, and the San Diego Chargers. He plays against them at least twice every year. There are other teams that are not as familiar, and one of them is the Philadelphia Eagles, the Raiders' opponents in Philadelphia on November 21.

What do I know about the Philadelphia Eagles? I can't even tell you who many of their players are. I know their quarterbacks because I check their statistics every week. And I know who some of their receivers are. I never played against them. We haven't played them since I've been with the Raiders. Maybe we played them when I wasn't the starting quarterback but that doesn't count.

Back in those days, when I was sitting on the bench, I really didn't give a damn who the other team was. I've played against some of the Philadelphia players when they were with other teams. I remember Bill Bergey, the linebacker, from when he was playing for Cincinnati. He's a good football player. And I know Blenda Gay. He used to be with the Raiders or at least he was in training camp.

I've watched films of the Eagles but I didn't watch for specific players. You watch what they do rather than who they are. I can tell you the numbers of their defensive backs because those are the guys I watch the closest in the films. But I really am not sure of their names.

Philadelphia is supposed to be a very rough team. We could see that in the films when they were playing other teams. I think Bill Bergey gives them that reputation. He's a helluva football player. He's big, about 250, and plays rough. He isn't dirty but he's rough and you know when he hits you. He can hurt.

They may not be any rougher than other teams in the league but sometimes one player can give them a reputation of being a rough team, and Bergey does that for Philadelphia. I've never had any run-ins with him. Thank God for that. He's a mean guy. He takes his job very seriously, which is the way it should be. I don't really care how hard a guy tackles me as long as it's clean. Well, I don't like to get hit too hard but that's part of the game. Bergey is a very emotional football player, and that's why he is so good. If you don't play the game with emotion, you might as well not play.

You can see on a film how a guy plays. You see a good play and you wonder who made it. Who was that guy—number 60? Then you see him do it again and you know he's a good player. That's the way it is with Bergey. He's the key to the whole Philadelphia defense. If we block Bergey, we'll be able to run the ball against the Eagles. That's the way most teams have beat Philadelphia this season, by running the ball.

Passing is another thing. If we have to do that instead of running, I think we can do it. We should be able to beat them. Just because I say that, they'll probably kill us. But I think we should win. We have a pretty good idea what we can do against Philadelphia. If they play the way they have in the films, there are some things we know we can do against them.

There are some teams that try to avoid the best player on the other team. If he's a linebacker like Bergey, they'll run their plays away from him. But we won't do that because we don't think we can avoid him. He's so damn quick for a big guy that he goes wherever the ball is. We'll go right at him and maybe wear him down. We'll just keep blocking him and running right at him. If we can beat him, we can beat the Eagles.

If you try to avoid him, run plays away from him, he'll go with the flow of the play. If he gets a good start at one of our ball carriers like that, he could take someone's life. He's that tough. We don't have anything special for him. Our game plan is always to try to beat the best players on the other team. If we can do that, it breaks their spirit. They realize that if we go after their good people and make yards, then we can do almost anything we want.

We're a straight-ahead team. We don't do too many fancy things. Our offensive line is the best in the league and they can block anyone. I have confidence in them. If one of our guards like George Buehler, who weighs about 270 pounds, can't handle a linebacker one-on-one, we're in trouble. But I have no doubt in my mind that Buehler can handle even a guy as good as Bergey. He outweighs him by 20 or 30 pounds and should be able to block him on straight-ahead plays. That's why you don't try to avoid people on other teams.

We'll put our strength against their strength. And I think we've got the best team in the league. The only time we might avoid a player is a defensive end. If we know a guy is real good, like Cedrick Hardman of the San Francisco 49ers, we might run our plays to the other side because it's easier. You can do that when the guy plays on one side or the other.

You can't do it when he's a middle linebacker. What we try to do sometimes is fool them. We'll have a misdirect play that looks like one thing but really is something else. After we do that once or twice, the defensive man has to hesitate for a second before he makes his move. That's all the time we need to make the play work. I watch for things like that when we're looking at movies of another team we're going to play. But when I'm watching a football game on TV, I watch it like any other fan.

Hell, I just watch the ball-carrier. I don't look to see who is blocking who or what the defense is doing. I just try to enjoy the game. There are times I'll second-guess the quarterback when I'm watching a game on TV. I'll say to myself that I would have called a different play in a certain situation. I'm just like the guy sitting in a bar having a beer and watching the game. I think they should pass when they run but it doesn't make any difference what I think.

I'll say to myself, "Why did he call that play? I

don't think I would have called it in that situation." But mostly I just enjoy the game. If the team I'm rooting for is losing, I might be wondering why they don't do something different.

Even if I'm watching a pro game, like Monday night TV, I don't pay that much attention to what a team is doing even if we're going to play them the next week. I figure they will probably be doing different things against us. When we look at a film of a team we're going to play, we look for certain things and the coaches tell us what to look for. That's when football is work. When I'm watching a game on TV, I'm just enjoying it like anyone else.

I sit there and watch and think that here's a situation where I would throw a long pass to Cliff Branch or maybe throw a short one to Dave Casper. If you're a quarterback, you're always thinking about things like that. But hell, it doesn't mean anything. It's just a way to enjoy the game a little more.

I watch every game I can on TV. I'll watch anything that is sports. I don't care if it's basketball or baseball or hockey. I'll even watch the bowling shows or *Wide World of Sports*. I love to watch sports on television.

I don't go to games in person unless I'm playing in them. The last time I remember going to a game as a spectator was about 1969.

I don't like to sit there in the stands and hear what the fans say about the players. I start thinking that they don't know what they're talking about and I want to tell them. But I can't do that so I don't go. I couldn't go to a game and just sit there. Maybe I could after I quit playing but not now. I don't like the idea of fighting the crowd. Because I'm Ken

Stabler there is no way I can enjoy a game if I'm sitting in the stands.

I went to a high school game last season to see our trainer George Anderson's son play. He's good and plays for Pinole Valley. They were playing a good team and I wanted to see his kid play. But I didn't get the chance. Someone saw me and everyone came over for autographs. It seemed like everyone in a whole section came over to where I was sitting. I couldn't enjoy the game. They just stood around. I must have signed autographs for an hour and a half.

That's why I don't go to games in person. If I go I want to see it and people won't let you. They don't realize that they're bothering you. I wouldn't even go the Super Bowl if I wasn't playing in it. I wouldn't walk across the street to see it. Last year I watched about half of it on TV. But then I got depressed. I kept thinking the Raiders should be playing in it instead of the Pittsburgh Steelers.

The year before I watched the whole Super Bowl on TV. I'm not sure why. There must not have been anything else to do or nothing else on TV.

Once our football season is over, that's it for me. You still have to live with what has happened and because of the way the season has ended for us the last few years, that's not very pleasant.

Post-season games don't interest me unless it's Alabama playing in it. I'll always watch then.

You can't put football completely out of your mind at the end of the season but you don't want to be reminded of things you don't like. Like losing to Pittsburgh.

I don't mind talking about football after the season is over. You can't shut it out completely. I don't mind talking football with fans who are fairly knowledgeable. I enjoy people who ask good questions. But I get kind of tired of the ones who ask how old George Blanda is or how tall Ben Davidson is.

I know people are interested in that but they don't have to ask me about it. I would rather have them ask me why we didn't beat Pittsburgh in the playoffs. I figure I know something about that. Football is my life so I enjoy talking about it. It would be the same with a lawyer. Suppose he said he didn't want to talk about law when he wasn't at his job?

You can't shut out your job even when you're away from it. But I don't talk about it all the time either. I try to rest sometimes and get away from football.

There are some people who do bother me. Hell, they think because we're the Oakland Raiders we're better than any other team in football. We might be but they don't understand that we have to work hard to win games. The games we have left should be easy if we play the way we can. But people look at our schedule and see that we play Philadelphia and Tampa Bay and San Diego. They think they're patsies. That's bullshit.

A guy from Tampa Bay can hurt you just as much as a guy from Pittsburgh. People don't seem to understand that one team doesn't have an easier schedule than another one. They look at a team's record last year and think they'll be bad this year. New England was a bad team in 1975 and they're a very good team this year. That's what I mean.

When the schedule for this season came out, it looked like we had some easy games. But we really don't. There are some teams we should beat but that doesn't mean it will be easy. We never go into a game figuring the other team is going to lie down and give us the game. Tampa Bay is an expansion team but their players want to win as much as anyone else. I'm not a very nervous person but I'm just as concerned about playing Philadelphia or Tampa Bay as I am about playing the Steelers.

I'll go into the Philadelphia game as if we're playing Pittsburgh. We want to win all our games. After a half, we might have a chance to make the game easy. But it isn't that way when it starts. All our players feel the same way. It's tough to tell Clarence Davis, our halfback, that Philadelphia is an easy game when he has to block Bill Bergey. Clarence weighs about 195 and Bergey is about 250. You think that's easy for him?

There are upsets every week. That's because some teams don't take the other team as seriously as they should. Hell, that's what happened when we played New England early in the season. Everyone thought it would be an easy game and they killed us.

Sometimes records don't mean a damn. We have to go out and win every Sunday. We're not going to win just because we're the Oakland Raiders. We get teams like San Diego who always give us trouble. We're a better team than they are but they always make it tough on us.

You get your bumps and bruises no matter who you play. It's a tough game. You take a physical beating when you play pro football. Or at least you take the chance of getting beat up.

I'm lucky because I play a position where I don't get hit on every play.

I'm speaking for the other guys on our team—the guard who has to block a big guy on every play or the ball-carrier who gets hit hard every time he runs the ball. Or the wide receiver who never knows when he's going to get hit.

We expect a tough game from Philadelphia but we also expect to win.

The Raiders defeated the Philadelphia Eagles, 26–7, but they found it difficult to avoid Bill Bergey. The Philadelphia linebacker made nine tackles and helped out on 10 others.

"We took what they gave us," Stabler said. "We didn't take anything for granted. Bill Bergey? I think he showed what a great football player he is."

Stabler completed 14 of 18 passes for 133 yards and one touchdown. And he did not get sacked by Bill Bergey.

16

The Protectors

The Oakland Raiders are considered to have one of the best offensive lines in professional football. Their main job is to protect quarterback Ken Stabler. Typically in pro football, the names of Oakland's offensive linemen are not household words. But Stabler knows, and appreciates, the talents of the six men who protect him. They are center Dave Dalby, guards Gene Upshaw and George Buehler, tackles John Vella and Art Shell, and tight end Dave Casper.

Without a good offensive line, a quarterback is nothing. If he doesn't get time to throw the ball, he's never going to complete a pass. We have a helluva offensive line. They give me time to throw the ball and that's why I complete passes and we win.

They don't get near enough credit for the job they

do. I know it and the coaches know it and they know it but the fans in the stands don't realize how important they are to the success of a football team. Dave Dalby, the center, is kind of the key to the whole thing. He's the one who sets the huddle and that's very important to the organization of the offense. You see some other teams where the center is wandering around after the play is over. Dave always knows where the ball is going to be spotted and then he sets up our huddle where it should be. It's one of the little things that separates a winning team from a losing team.

Dalby may not be all-pro but he's a football player who takes pride in doing a good job. Ollie Spencer, our offensive line coach, says the same thing about him. I've seen Dalby play when he was hurting. That's the sign of a player who is proud. They don't want to come out of a game because they think that means they can't do the job.

I've seen times when Dalby is really hurtin' but he still hustles on every play. He's the first guy back to where the huddle will be. After I call the play, he claps his hands and breaks the huddle. I like a guy who does that. I like a guy who's always yelling and clapping when he comes out of the huddle. I notice things like that because it's good for team spirit. He's tough and he's smart. Most people think offensive linemen don't have to be smart but that isn't true. There are times when the center has to call plays on the line of scrimmage.

If I call an audible, then Dalby has to change the blocking assignments in the line. And he has to do it quick. If I call a play and then change it by calling an audible like "69," then Dalby has to call "Rip" or "Liz" or whatever key word it is that changes the blocking. He has to know almost as much as the quarterback.

There are no dummies in pro football, at least not in the offensive line. You have to be smart and a quick thinker if you want to play there. Fans wonder why rookies don't usually become starters in the offensive line. That's why. There is so damn much to learn that it takes time.

Rookies usually start on defense because that's where you react to something that happens. On offense the linemen are the ones who make things happen. There are times when Dave will forget the snap number and center the ball at the wrong time. But everyone does that.

Hell, I've done it myself. I call for the ball on "three" in the huddle and then I'll get up there at the line of scrimmage and expect it on "one." I'll jump out of there and won't have the ball. Dalby doesn't make mistakes very often. That's why he's such a great center.

Gene Upshaw is the holler guy of our offensive line. He's the cheerleader . . . a politician. He's always talking about something. He has said that he wants to run for public office and that's what it seems like he's doing in the locker room sometimes. He walks around and acts like he's a politician. He's always picking at someone and jawing with them—not in a mean way. He just likes to talk. Gene is always saying this or that and never shuts up. But I like to have at least one guy around like that. As long as it's just one.

He keeps things going in the huddle. When he feels good there isn't a better guy to have around. It's always good things he says. Rah-rah stuff. You know, some people think that's just for college teams but I like to see a little bit of it on a pro team too. Gene is our cheerleader. He's played a long time, and he's made all-pro a bunch of times. It isn't as if all he did was talk. He's a damn fine player to go along with his talk.

I've never seen a guard as big as he is, about 260 or 270 pounds, who can run like Upshaw can. He gets out there in front of those halfbacks and that's tough to do. He's a helluva pulling guard. He's also a finesse player. He isn't an overpowering guy for his size on straight-ahead bucks or pass protection. He uses finesse. He won't just fire out like George Buehler, who crushes the other guy with physical strength. Upshaw will try to figure out how he can finesse the guy he has to block. He'll try to fool him and he gets the job done that way.

If he can't fool them or finesse them, then he crushes them with his size and strength. When he gets out there on a sweep, he can bury a defensive back who comes up to try to make the tackle. That's where Upshaw is really impressive, on the sweeps. Then, after the play is over, he'll come back to the huddle and start talking. He'll be telling you he can do this or that. And he'll be telling the other linemen to remember to do certain things.

He talks to them but he doesn't talk to me very much. He might be reminding Art Shell about a blocking combination they are working on. He's the talker on the offensive line but I never have to tell him to knock it off. He knows there's a time to talk and a time not to. When we're standing up waiting for the ball to be spotted, I don't care who talks. Once we get down, all that bullshit is over. I'm the one who does the talking.

Art Shell is a proud guy. What I like about him is how much it bothers him when his man beats him and gets to me. That doesn't happen too often because Art is such a great tackle. But when it does, you can tell it bothers him. A couple years ago Art was blocking John Zook of the Atlanta Falcons and Zook got by him and hit me late. Shell took off after Zook and tried to get him. He was mad because Zook beat him and because he hit me late. That made me feel good to see one of my teammates do that for me. Art Shell didn't get the recognition he deserved for a long time. He was so damn good and consistent that people didn't notice him.

Some tackles make a great block on one play and then get beat on the next one. Art is great all the time. He's one of the best offensive tackles in the league. He's smart on the blocking combinations and is always working to get better. He tries to figure out how to handle his man in each game. He watches the films to see what kind of moves his man has. Then he gets ready for him. The only time Art has trouble is when he goes against a guy who is smaller and quicker than he is. Art is big. He must weigh 290 or 300 pounds. He'll tell you he weighs about 270 but he's closer to 300. The program says he weighs 265 but I know he's much bigger than that.

If he gets against a guy who is quicker, he'll study his moves and be ready for him. He knows if the guy takes an inside charge or comes on the outside. Art works at being a smart blocker. The only time he ever says anything in the huddle is when he needs help on a block, and that isn't very often. If we're going to run a draw play to his side, he might ask to have the tight end on that side to help because it's a tough block he has to make. It isn't that he always needs the help but he knows the play will work better if he does have. That's what I mean about him knowing his job and being a smart player.

When he needs something he asks for it and I respect that. On some teams, there are guys who are always asking for help on blocks. The only time Shell asks is to make the play go better. He gets help when he asks for it. Last week Art hurt his shoulder and it was really bad. He didn't want to go out of the game and he needed help on some of his blocks. I made sure he got it.

Other guys will just bite the bullet when they get hurt and then they get beat by their man. That isn't smart. You have to know when you need help. That's the way Art Shell is.

George Buehler is what an offensive guard in the NFL should be. If he were a mean guy or an emotional guy, they would have to outlaw him. Oh God, is he strong. He's probably the strongest player, pound for pound, in pro football. He could turn over a truck. He's got those huge legs, huge arms, and a thick neck. He's a bull. He's built like a Coke machine with a head on top of it. He weighs 270 pounds and doesn't have any stomach—just those huge arms, legs, and neck.

If you had to make a mold for an offensive lineman, George Buehler is the guy you would use for the model. He has the perfect build for it. He's so easygoing and he's a very religious person. I would hate to see what would happen if he ever got mad at someone. George is the kind of guy who would apologize if he stepped on someone's toe while he was blocking his man. He would go over to the guy and say, "I'm sorry I stepped on your toe." That's the way he is.

He has bull strength and draws most of the top defensive tackles to play against. When we play Pittsurgh, he gets Mean Joe Greene. When we play Houston, he gets Curley Culp. It seems like most of the top defensive linemen in the league are left tackles and Buehler has to block them. Paul Smith of Denver and Merlin Olsen of the Rams are other guys he gets. He seldom gets called for penalties because he's so strong his man doesn't beat him very often.

He has less holding penalties than anyone else on our team. That's because he will do anything he can to keep from breaking the rules. There are times when I can understand a guy holding. If he gets beat by his man, he might grab to protect the quarterback from getting injured. But George would never do that. He's so damn honest that he follows the rules no matter what happens.

If George were walking along a dark street in the middle of the night, and he found a $100 bill, he would look for someplace to turn it in. Or he would wait right there where he found it until someone came along to claim it. I'd stick it in my pocket. What the hell, it's something you found. But not George Buehler. He just isn't that kind of guy.

George is real smart. He's a Stanford graduate. His father is a doctor and his brother is in medicine. George could have done the same but he wanted to play football. If he were a mean guy, or a rough guy, no one would be able to stop him.

John Vella, our right tackle, is a battler. He would start battling you at eight in the morning and would still be battling you when the sun went down if that's what it takes to win. That's the kind of guy he is.

He's hot-tempered and emotional. He's the exact opposite of Buehler. You notice that whenever one of our offensive linemen gets in a fight, it's always Joh Vella.

Think of all the fights you see and John is in all o the ones that we get in. He'll battle you any way h can. He's always scrapping and I wouldn't trade hin for anyone else. I like a guy who plays the game wit emotion. John may have trouble blocking some guy but he'll never ask for help. He's too proud for that He might hold the guy if that's what it takes to sto him. He'll stop him any way he can. When we playe Los Angeles, Vella was having trouble with Jac Youngblood but he didn't ask for help. He just kep playing hard and battling, and then he stopped him.

He'll fight if he has to. He doesn't talk much in th huddle and neither does Buehler. They might tal about their blocking combinations but that's all. The talk business and that's the way it should be.

Dave Casper, our tight end, might be the smartes guy in the line. He's a golden domer—you know, fron Notre Dame. He's always trying to figure out some thing that will help us. He's our "thinking man's re ceiver." He knows what the other team's coverage is And he knows what to do against it. I'll call a pla and he'll come up with something that will work eve better.

I don't resent that because I know he is sure it's better way. He doesn't do it that often but if h thinks he has a better way to do something, he'll te me about it. He really blossomed this season when h became a regular. The ball is coming his way and he' catching it. Hell, he's caught 34 passes already. Yo can't knock that. Russ Francis, the tight end fron New England, may have more speed than Caspe does but he can't catch the ball as well. Casper doe verything well. He's a very popular player on our eam.

But he's the worst-looking player I've ever seen in ractice. He looks bad when he's running and warmng up. He can't catch the ball in practice, but doesn't niss it once the game starts. To me, he looks like he von't come in out of the rain. When he's warming up, ou look at him and think that every step he takes is oing to be his last.

You'd think that he was on his last legs. You expect im to fall down, but once the game starts and the all is snapped, there isn't a better tight end in footall. Once the game starts he's spectacular. I guess hat's the way it should be.

Two days later the Raiders went out and whipped he Tampa Bay Buccaneers, 49–16. The offensive line rotected Stabler well enough to allow him to comlete 15 of 23 passes for 245 yards and two touchlowns. John Vella didn't get in any fights and only nce was a Tampa Bay lineman able to get to Stabler.

17

Al Davis' Pressure Cooker

Opposites attract. And there are no more opposite people in pro football than quarterback Ken Stabler and managing general partner Al Davis of the Oakland Raiders.

Stabler is a good 'ol boy from Foley, Alabama. He is pleasant, outgoing, and candid.

Al Davis grew up on the sidewalks of Brooklyn. He is enterprising, shrewd, and has been known to bend rules to get what he wants.

It is Wednesday and the Raiders are working out at their Alameda training camp, preparing for the Monday night game against the Cincinnati Bengals on December 6. The practice is devoted to offense, which means Stabler is the center of attention. He calls the plays and throws the passes that he expects will beat the Bengals.

Lurking along the sidelines is Al Davis. He doesn't miss a thing. Wide receiver Cliff Branch runs a pass pattern without the proper cut.

"Cliff," Davis says in a barely audible voice. "When you run that pattern, make the cut sharp. That way the defensive back can't anticipate what you are going to do next."

Branch nods his head and goes back to the huddle. The Branch-Davis conversation has not escaped the attention of Ken Stabler.

Does Al Davis know football? He really impresses me with some things he says. You wouldn't believe some of the things he comes up with. He's a super-smart man who really knows how to manipulate people . . . and players.

If you are not careful you'll come up on the short end when you're dealing with him. He knows how to keep players from going to other teams and how to keep players for himself.

But football? He's never satisfied. And he's a second-guesser. I don't like that. I remember a game earlier in the season when I threw a touchdown pass. There were two receivers open. When I came off the field, Davis wanted to know why I didn't throw to the other receiver. He's never satisfied. Maybe that's the way to run a business because he's been very successful.

It doesn't make any difference if you win. He'll still find something wrong. If you lose he'll tell you what you did wrong. But he never does it in front of anyone else and I appreciate that. I guess that's his way of striving for excellence.

That's one of the things I have learned from Al Davis. Never be satisfied with your performance. It can always be better. He demands a lot from people. He demands a lot from players and from his staff. He demands a lot from me. I've always produced for him and won. The only thing I haven't done is win the Super Bowl. That's one thing we have in common. We both want that more than anything else.

Al Davis is worried about the game with Cincinnati. He isn't worried about winning. He is more concerned with talk that the Raiders might lose the game intentionally to keep Pittsburgh out of the playoffs.

A reporter asks Davis about the rumors of "dumping" the game.

"Fuck," he says with a southern accent picked up the year he was an assistant coach at the Citadel in South Carolina. "How can anyone say that . . . I mean . . . Fuck . . . Don't they think we want to win the game and have the best record and be the home team in the playoffs? We don't care who we play after we get in the playoffs."

I've heard the talk about dumping the game. I talked to Fred Biletnikoff and Pete Banaszak about it. We all feel the same way. We're professional athletes. Every time we go out on the field we play our best. How could we do anything else?

That's bullshit that we wouldn't try. It's Pittsburgh trying to stir things up. They always do.

Stabler and Davis have what might be called a "fragile" relationship.

I know some day my day will come. I'm trying not to let it happen . . . to let Davis get the upper hand.

I've seen what he has done to people and I don't like it.

I guess the only time I really had trouble with Al Davis was when I signed with Birmingham of the World Football League. He wasn't mad. He was hurt that I would do that without talking to him. The way I did it probably wasn't right. Instead of going and talking to him, and telling him about the offer I had from Birmingham, and that I would like to play for them, I just went ahead and signed.

I should have told him I wanted to play for Birmingham because it was near my home. I should have given him a shot at offering the same money they did. I still feel bad that I didn't do things the right way. But I did it and now I have to live with it. That's why I say my day could come in dealing with Al Davis. After I do what I have to do with the Raiders, then I better watch my Ps and Qs.

Al Davis can be very impressive. He's done a lot in a few years. He started out as an assistant coach in college, he was an assistant coach in the pros, and then a head coach. Then one day he was the commissioner of the American Football League, and now he's the owner of a team that's worth about $20 million.

That's a long way to come in about 10 or 12 years. I know there are some people who question how he got where he is . . . if he did it the right way. But you have to respect him for doing it. He could probably be the commissioner of the National Football League if he really wanted to be.

They say Al Davis scares people. But he doesn't scare me. Some people get respect from fear. Al Davis may do that too. But I respect him for what he has accomplished—even though I might not like the way he has treated people to get where he is.

If you do something against him or his organization, he doesn't forget. If a sportswriter writes something he doesn't like, the writer won't travel with the team anymore. I've seen that happen. If a player plays out his option and tries to go somewhere else, then that player gets cut or is out of football.

Al Davis is that powerful. People just don't cross him and get away with it. That's why other owners don't like to do business with him. He always comes out on top. You're subject to getting screwed when you deal with Al Davis.

What I like about Al is his dedication to making the Oakland Raiders the Super Bowl champions. It's unbelievable. If we ever do win the Super Bowl, he'll give the players the moon. He'll outdo anything that has ever been done before. He'll give us the biggest rings you ever saw.

If we don't win, he'll just try harder the next year until we finally do win the Super Bowl. It isn't what you have done for him that matters with Al Davis. It's what you can do for him today or tomorrow. I've seen it happen to other players . . . Billy Cannon . . . George Blanda and Clem Daniels. Once they couldn't help the Raiders anymore, they were gone. The same thing could happen to me.

That's the nature of pro football and that's the way Al Davis runs his business.

He's a shrewd man, and I like that about him. He didn't just fall off a turnip truck. He's been around and knows what's going on. I enjoy playing for him. I really do.

Does Davis, as some critics have suggested, call the plays for head coach John Madden?

No, I'm sure he doesn't. Madden doesn't even call plays for me. We talk about what might go and everyone makes suggestions. But once we're on the field it's up to me. At practice, Davis makes suggestions. I'm sure he has private meetings with the coaches. He has some ideas on what he wants us to do. Whether John Madden does those things is something else. I think John calls his own shots. They get together on the game plan. They incorporate everyone's ideas into it.

We had a coach here during my rookie year—John Rauch. He was successful. He got the team to the Super Bowl in 1968 but then the next season he just kind of disappeared. I remember that and I'm sure Al Davis had something to do with it. Rauch didn't listen to Davis so he was gone.

That's another reason I respect John Madden so much. He's under tremendous pressure from Al Davis. He has to win. It's just like there is pressure on the players to win. If you don't produce, you're gone. That's why I'm still here. I have produced. That's why John Madden is still here. He's produced. And that's why Al Davis is here.

The only thing none of us has done is win the Super Bowl. That's why we're still here together. All three of us need that real bad. Hell, it's all I ever think about. I've done everything else there is to do in football. I guess Al Davis and John Madden have too. And I respect John Madden for the pressure he has been under working for Al Davis all these years.

When it comes to applying pressure, Al Davis can really do it.

There are some people who suggest that Al Davis is ruthless . . . that he will do anything to win.

I think you could say that. Maybe he doesn't realize it when he steps on people. Maybe he doesn't realize that they have feelings. It doesn't matter to him as long as he gets what he wants. What he wants is to have the best football team in the world and he's close to having it.

Maybe that's why he does the things he does. He can really manipulate players and I don't appreciate that. He keeps bringing in players . . . good players. Some are troublemakers, or at least they are supposed to be, but they don't cause any trouble for Al Davis. If they do, they don't stay around. All I can say is he has to be doing something right. His record is second to none in pro football.

On a cool Monday night, the Oakland Raiders play the Cincinnati Bengals in a game clouded with controversy. The Raiders don't waste any time letting their fans know they have come to play.

Stabler throws two touchdown passes to tight end Dave Casper in the first quarter to give the Raiders a 14–6 lead. Pete Banaszak busts over for a touchdown in the second quarter for a 21–13 halftime lead. Stabler passes to Cliff Branch for 42 yards and another touchdown in the third quarter and then hits Fred Biletnikoff from seven yards out for his fourth scoring pass of the night.

Stabler is 16 of 20 in the game for 217 yards and four touchdowns. And Oakland wins, 35–20.

I think we shut some people up. People said we were scared of certain teams. That's bullshit. We're not scared of any team. Cincinnati is a good team and we beat them. We didn't lay down like some people said we would. We didn't need motivation to win. We can beat anyone in the league.

As he talked with reporters in his corner of the dressing room, Stabler caught the eye of Davis, lurking in another corner. They exchanged a sly smile. The kid from Foley, Alabama, and the man from Brooklyn were one step closer to their goal.

18

Monday Night TV

Ken Stabler likes to watch Monday night football. But on December 6 he was otherwise occupied. He, and his teammates, were themselves on the tube—as opponents of the Cincinnati Bengals. Ken was thus in no position to react to the telecasting trio of Howard Cosell, Alex Karras, and Frank Gifford. But he has strong opinions on this controversial team.

Everyone wants to be impressive in a Monday night game because everyone watches. I thought about my coaches—high school and college—who would be watching and wanted to play good for them.

And also a lot of my friends and relatives who don't see me much anymore. But other than that it's just another game. Cosell? He seems to say nice things about whichever team is the best. He's a front-runner.

Whoever is going good is his favorite team. I've talked with him several times. He's a showman and the game is entertainment.

His total recall is very impressive. But that's part of his act. He seems to think people turn on the game to see him instead of the teams that are playing. He rattles off all this information about the players. He studies up on things like that but he doesn't know that much about football. I don't agree with a lot of the things he says because I think I know what a team is trying to do.

You have to play a game to know what is going on. It may look like a player isn't doing his job but how can Cosell tell if he doesn't know what the player's job is? He raps players who probably don't deserve it and he praises players when they don't deserve it. The players know that. But I guess the fans are impressed with what he says. That telling-it-like-it-is crap isn't much if you don't know football.

Gifford? He just tells what is happening. You never hear him knocking anyone because he has played football. Maybe he realizes what is going on. Cosell and Gifford are a good combination. Howard is show business and Gifford talks about the game.

Alex Karras? I guess he's supposed to be funny. But he doesn't know football. A blocking dummy knows as much about football as he does. He just isn't informed. At the start of our game with Cincinnati, he said he didn't think we would try too hard. He said we were not interested in winning. We blew Cincinnati out and they have a good team. So what does Karras do? Later in the game he says we seem to be playing well. I'll give him credit for that but he shouldn't have said what he did in the first place.

That's the kind of stuff that gets to a player. Monday night football can do a lot for a player both ways. If Cosell says someone is good, a lot of people watching think he is, even if he isn't. The same goes for someone he knocks. That can have an effect on sportswriters who don't see the Raiders play. They vote for all-pro teams and it might be because of what Cosell said rather than how good a player really is. That's the bad part of it.

Cosell can make you sound like Clark Kent if he thinks you are good. He may think you're the greatest thing since sliced bread. Monday night football is a big thing. But it isn't as big as Howard Cosell makes it. Football was played for a long time before he discovered it.

I don't like to play night games. It doesn't fit into the regular routine. You have all day to kill before the game. Take the Cincinnati game. I woke up at nine o'clock and went to a short meeting. It was films of the Bengals playing the Houston Oilers. I had seen it about 300 times before.

I really didn't watch because I knew how it was going to come out. The only thing I watched was the quarterbacks who were playing against the Bengals. Dan Pastorini. I watched to see what he called in certain situations and what the Bengals did. But that doesn't help me because I might never be in the same situation. I'm a different kind of quarterback.

Besides, if you don't know what you're going to do by 11 o'clock on the morning of the game, it's too late. Watching films won't help you. After the meeting I went home to Danville and fed my horses. We have about four acres out there. Then I played with my dog for a while.

We had a pregame meal early in the afternoon—steak and eggs, and I had some hot tea. Steak and eggs? Some people had ham and eggs. You can have whatever you want. Some guys have chicken or ribs.

We had to be back at the stadium at 4:30. I don't get excited about a game then. I really don't get excited until the opening kickoff. After the meal I went back to my room at the Hilton Hotel (about a mile from the stadium) and watched TV. I think the show was "Tattle Tales." I don't particularly like the show but that was what was on. Then I slept for an hour. I was relaxed.

Like I say, I don't get excited until the game starts. I got to the stadium on time. It wasn't a playoff game but there seemed to be more excitement than for other games. Maybe it was all the talk about us lying down and not trying to win. The fans were sure excited. You could feel it. The place was buzzing. But all I wanted to do was rest and keep cool. I wasn't thinking about the game even after I got in the locker room.

We had discussed the Pittsburgh thing during the week. I remember talking to John Vella about it. But there was never anything about not trying. You don't have to tell a pro athlete to try. It was a big joke that we would try to lose the game to get Pittsburgh out of the playoffs.

Wouldn't it be funny, if after all this talk, that the Steelers lost to Houston and didn't make the playoffs after all? (Pittsburgh beat Houston, 32–16.)

We decided we would play the game with Cincinnati our way—just like any other game. We take our games one at a time and Cincinnati is just the 13th game of the season. We want to win every time we go on the field. After all, a 13–1 record ain't bad.

The Cincinnati game plan? We wanted to throw short passes under their coverage. They have the best pass defense in the conference. We saw other teams do it so we tried to do the same. Then, we wanted to establish a running game because that helps make the passing game go. We wanted to control the ball and felt that we could. Then we could hit a couple big ones and that would be it.

I guess I could have completed every pass I threw with some luck. What was I, 16 of 20? The first pass was not too good. I threw it short because Freddie Biletnikoff and I got mixed up about where he was supposed to be. Then there was the one to Casper. That was my fault. He had a chance to catch it because he made a great try. But it was not a good throw.

If we were lucky he might have caught it. The long one to Branch could have been caught. He can do it. I think it was deflected just a little but he still had it in his hands. 20 for 20 would really have been something.

Someone will do it. I've completed 15 in a row. Against Baltimore I had 15 in a row and then there were two more completions that the officials said were out of bounds. But the movies showed that they weren't. That might have been a perfect day.

I really don't ever expect to complete every pass I throw. I can see where a quarterback like Ken Anderson or Bert Jones might do it. They dump the ball off to the running backs a lot. I don't do that much. We throw the ball down the field and that way it's a little harder to complete passes.

Completing all my passes wouldn't be that big a deal. I would rather pass for 400 yards in a game. That would really be something. I never did it in college or high school because I didn't throw that much then. The only thing about passing for 400 yards is you have to throw the ball a lot. That means you have to and it might be because you are behind. You would be throwing instead of running to do it.

If we could win the game and I could still pass for 400 yards, that would be all right. But I would never put personal goals ahead of the team. That's a small goal—the 400 yards. But it is something I would like to do. Can you imagine that Norm Van Brocklin passed for 554 yards in one game? That must have been something.

Touchdown passes are something else. I would like to have five in a game if it meant that it helped us win and we weren't pouring it on the other team. I've had four in a game quite a few times but never five.

After the Cincinnati game, I talked to Anderson. I always try to shake hands with the other quarterback. He wished us luck in the playoffs. It seemed like they had given up. They didn't expect to make the playoffs.

I also said hello to Jim LeClair, their linebacker. I had never met him before. But I had been looking across the line at him for three hours so I thought I would say hello. He told me we had a helluva team.

I didn't talk to Coy Bacon. There were a couple times during the game when I winked at him. One time I threw a pass and he had a chance to hit me late. But he didn't. He kind of smiled and I winked. He knew what I meant. I didn't have to say anything. Then another time I did the same thing. I want to have a good rapport with all the defensive players. That's the way the game should be played.

I was happy that Mark van Eeghen played well. He's going to be a good fullback for a long time. He really works hard. He's quick for a guy who weighs 225 pounds. He's an intense player. He never quits trying. He gets keyed up when he plays and sometimes that hurts him. On screen passes he starts to run before he has the ball. But he'll get better. I really want him to get his 1,000 yards. We'll try to get it for him. Going into the final game of the season van Eeghen needs 83 yards to reach 1,000 for the first time in his career.

That plateau means a lot to him. That's the way they measure the ability of running backs. He gets some good runs. He doesn't break away for 70 or 80 yards in one pop like O. J. Simpson. But he gets 8 and 6. He makes up for other things with great desire. He also is a good blocker. He never says anything in the huddle. No one does very often. No one seems surprised at the plays I call. We're 12–1, so I must know what's going on.

I've said all along that we will get better and peak in the playoffs. That hasn't happened before. I think it will this season.

19

Three to Go

The Oakland Raiders completed the regular season with a 24–0 romp over the San Diego Chargers. They finished with a 13–1 record, the best in the entire National Football League. That earned them the home-field advantage in the American Conference playoffs and their first opponent will be the New England Patriots December 18 at Oakland Coliseum.

After the way New England had kicked the hell out of us early in the season (48–17), I guess I should have been worried about meeting the Pats in the playoffs. But I wasn't.

The first part of the game was a defensive battle. They got the kickoff and couldn't do much. Neither could we the first time we had the ball. Then their quarterback, Steve Grogan, started throwing the ball and took them right down the field. The big play was a 40-yard pass to their tight end, Russ Francis. Our defensive back, George Atkinson, made the tackle . . . and that was what everyone talked about afterwards: how Atkinson broke Francis's nose with a clothesline tackle.

Francis outweighs Atkinson by about 40 pounds and George had to stop him any way he could. It was get it on or get beat. He didn't do anything illegal. He had one shot at Francis, and when Francis ducked his head George hit him across the face with his arm. There was no penalty on the play, so how can it be dirty?

Football is a violent game. It's a physical thing and you have to fish or cut bait. It wasn't meant to be played in shorts and a T-shirt.

Right after the pass, Grogan threw another one—to Darryl Stingley—for 24 yards down to our one. Andy Johnson scored from there.

We came back to get a field goal after I missed on two passes and it was 7–3 at the end of the first quarter. That was still a lot better than the first time we played them. We couldn't do much in the second quarter. We lost the ball once on a fumble but got it back when they tried a trick play and Skip Thomas intercepted a pass by Francis.

We had about two minutes to go before the half so I started throwing the ball. I completed two to Dave Casper and then one to Fred Biletnikoff. We had the ball on their 31-yard line with 45 seconds to play. Freddie ran a great pattern into the right corner of the end zone and caught a pass for a touchdown. That put us ahead, 10–7, at the half.

They completely dominated the third quarter. They went 80 yards on one drive and Grogan passed to

Francis for the touchdown that put them ahead, 14–10. The next time they got the ball they scored again, this time on a run by Jess Phillips, who had started the season playing for us.

We went into the fourth quarter behind, 21–10, and I got to thinking maybe New England could beat us. I thought about all the work we had done during the season and now it seemed to be going down the drain. But we scored early in the fourth quarter (Mark van Eeghen from the one) to make it 21–17. We couldn't do anything the next time we got the ball and had to punt with a little more than six minutes to play.

They got to our 32-yard line by running the ball, we held, and they missed on a 50-yard field goal. If they had made it, we would have been in deep trouble. We got the ball with four minutes to play and I told the guys in the huddle it might be the last time we had the ball all year. I figured the best thing to do was throw the ball on every play like we did when we came back to beat Pittsburgh in the season opener.

I completed four of five passes and we got down to the New England 19-yard line with little more than a minute to play. Mel Lunsford, their defensive tackle, got me for a nine-yard loss and that made it second and 18 to go. I missed on a pass to Casper and it was third down. I called a sideline pass to Carl Garrett but their backs were all over him. Just as I threw the ball, Ray Hamilton hit me across the face with his arm. He was going for the ball but he hit me after I threw it. They called it roughing the passer and we got a first down on the 13-yard line. It was a big break for us but he did hit me.

The Pats said he tipped-the ball, which would

make it no penalty. It's a judgment call by the official. He didn't think Hamilton tipped the ball. Besides, there should have been a penalty called on the Patriots for interfering with Garrett. They were all over him.

I threw to Casper for five yards and then we got four more on a run by Clarence Davis. Pete Banaszak gained a yard on third down. It was close for the first down but one of their players argued with the officials and they called an unsportsmanlike-conduct penalty that put the ball on the one-yard line with 30 seconds to play.

I gave it to Banaszak and he was stopped for no gain. We had 14 seconds left so I decided to use an option play that had worked against Cincinnati. I roll out to the left and either run or throw the ball to Dave Casper. I had Gene Upshaw blocking for me and he knocked down the only guy who had a chance to get me. I scored and we were now ahead, 24–21. There were only 10 seconds left and New England didn't have a chance to do anything before the game ended.

We didn't have much chance to celebrate because we knew we had to play Pittsburgh the next week for the AFC championship. We didn't expect an easy game with them. We knew that from the game we played against the Steelers in the season opener.

They've always been a thorn in our sides. They've picked our pockets a hundred times. Every time we play them there's a controversy about something. I don't worry about all that stuff—the lawsuits and the fines, and what their coach was saying about us. I knew I couldn't control it so I don't worry about things like that.

What I could control was how our offense did and

that's what I was concerned about. Scoring points and winning games is the only thing that matters for me. I thought about all the times we had played Pittsburgh and lost and figured maybe it wasn't in the stars for us ever to beat them in a playoff game.

But I didn't believe we couldn't beat them because we had already done it once this season. Pittsburgh is a good team. They have a great pass rush and their defensive backs are good. Those are the people on the other team I think about.

What I like about playing against the Steelers is that they bring out the best in me. I like to play in a game where you have to reach down for a little extra to win. You always have to do that when you play Pittsburgh in the playoffs.

I didn't think it would be a dirty game in spite of what they thought we did to them the first time we played. You can't play your best when you're thinking about things like that instead of concentrating on the game.

I didn't think the Pittsburgh players would worry about what happened in that first game either. I know that Mean Joe Greene said he would go after anyone who did anything dirty but he always says that. We have some guys who can take care of people like Joe Greene.

The game was very physical but not dirty. Our defense was super. We were out there to prove that Pittsburgh wasn't going to run all over us like they had in the past.

The Steelers didn't get a first down in the first quarter. They made eight yards total. Terry Bradshaw couldn't complete a pass. We didn't do much better but we did get a field goal after Hubie Ginn partially blocked a punt and we got the ball on their 38-yard line.

We got a break in the second quarter when Willie Hall intercepted a pass and returned it to the Steeler one-yard line. Clarence Davis scored from there and we were ahead, 10–0. That seemed to wake the Steelers up. They came right back and scored on a short run by Reggie Harrison after Bradshaw completed a long pass to John Stallworth and another to Lynn Swann.

That put them back in the game but we came right back and scored again. This time we did it on a play we put in just for the game. It was something we had used against Cincinnati but a little different. It's called Tight Blue, Near Right, 84 Cross. Warren Bankston comes into the game as an extra tight end in a goal-line situation. We had the ball on their four-yard line with a first down.

It worked perfectly. They didn't cover Bankston too close because they didn't expect him to be the receiver. He told me afterward that he didn't expect to be that open. He was all alone. All I had to do was get the ball to him. That put us ahead, 17–7, at the half and I felt confident.

Our defense was doing a helluva job. They didn't have Franco Harris and Rocky Bleier, who were injured, but our defense would have stopped them if they had played. We held them the first two times they had the ball in the third quarter and then we scored on a pass to Banaszak.

That made it 24–7 and Bradshaw started to throw the ball on every play after that. Without Harris and Bleier, he had to. He threw the ball 10 times in a row the next time they had the ball but Atkinson covered

Swann real good on the last two and we took over the ball on our 29-yard line.

Our defense held them the rest of the way and we won. They never did get a chance to run the final play of the game because there were fans all over the field. There were only nine seconds left and Pittsburgh couldn't have won anyway.

Beating them really capped off the season for us. It shut up a lot of people who said we couldn't win big games. We beat the hell out of Pittsburgh. They couldn't say we were lucky—like they were against us that one year. We worked for everything we got.

I don't think it really sank in until the next day that we were going to the Super Bowl. So many things had happened before to keep us from going. But you can't celebrate until you win the Super Bowl.

Hell, if we lose in the Super Bowl it's just like losing in the AFC title game or the first round of the playoffs. You haven't accomplished a damn thing.

Winning that last game is the bottom line in football.

That's why I guess we didn't celebrate as much as we might have. But we did celebrate. We threw the coaches in the showers and we had a big time in the dressing room. Hell, I celebrate if we win or lose. If we lose, I cry in my beer. If we win, I buy the drinks.

We raised hell that night after the game. We went out and had a few drinks . . . quite a few drinks. We partied for a long time. But in the back of our minds we still knew there was one more game to play. There would be time for a real celebration after that.

20

The Week That Was

The frustration was over for Ken Stabler as he sat in the lobby of the Marriott Hotel in Newport Beach, California. The Oakland Raiders had finally made it to the Super Bowl, mainly because of Stabler.

The Raiders would spend a week at Newport Beach getting ready for the Super Bowl against the Minnesota Vikings. It would be a busy week, a time of distractions that can affect the play of a football team in the biggest game of the year.

Stabler was aware of the circus atmosphere of a Super Bowl. He had been through similar weeks when his Alabama team played in the Orange, Sugar and Cotton Bowls.

The Super Bowl is everything people have made it out to be. The big thing is getting into it. Once you've done that, you can enjoy it a little.

I've heard people say it's just another game. But it's not just another game for us. Maybe that's because it was so damn tough for us to get here.

The atmosphere of the game takes over the whole Los Angeles area. That's all you hear on the radio or on television. That's all you read about in the papers. It has to be a really big game to take over a city as big as Los Angeles. I'm glad we're in Newport Beach, away from Los Angeles. It's kind of fun down here. But you have to make it that way.

I'm not going to get uptight about the game. When you do that, you hurt your chances of winning. I enjoy playing in big games. I liked playing in the bowl games when I was in college. I think big games bring out the best in a player. At least it does in me.

You just have to try to ignore the distracting things that go on during Super Bowl Week. Coach Madden told us not to fight it. Hell, we're here because we're the best team in our conference so we're going to enjoy it. We have to conform to the schedule. It isn't what we want to do. It's what the NFL wants us to do. There are press conferences, TV interviews, and stuff like that. But there isn't any sense fighting it. Teams that have done that ended up losing in the Super Bowl because they had other things on their mind.

The press conferences are really something. I didn't know there were that many writers in the country. We have to give them time. We have to answer the questions. It's usually the same questions over and over again.

"Do you think you can win?" Of course we do. "Do you think you can score against the Minnesota defense?" We can score against any team.

I don't think anyone has asked me a question I

hadn't heard before. Not all week. But you just sit there and be nice and answer. The one thing you can't forget is why you are here. I would rather be here answering dumb questions than watching the Super Bowl on television like 26 other teams are doing.

I've talked to some of the Minnesota players about all the distractions. They've been here three times before and feel the way I do. You can't let all the crap bother you. You have to roll with the punches. Then you go out and do what you have to do to get ready for the game.

Our team attitude has been very good. Coach Madden is the reason for that. He never lets us forget why we are here. He wants to win the Super Bowl as much as I do. Maybe more. No, I don't think anyone wants to win the Super Bowl more than I do.

All the stuff going on hasn't bothered us in practice. We've had some of the best practices we've had all season. I think the reason is that our players know why they are here.

There were lots of reasons not to be sharp in practice. The rain . . . the mud . . . and all the other stuff. It isn't the same as practicing on a familiar field. That makes a difference too. We were sharp in everything we did. The passing game was good, so was the running game. I just hope it carries over into the Super Bowl.

I like the practices. I like everything about the Super Bowl. This is what you work all season for. From the time we went to training camp in July it's all you think about. You run the wind sprints and bust your tail in the heat to get here. Once you make it, you enjoy it.

It's been a long haul. Training camp, then six preseason games and 14 regular-season games. After that we had the pressure of the two playoff games. We played 22 tough games to get here.

It's like a bowl game in college. But not quite the same. There wasn't as much media coverage for a college bowl game. I guess that's because there were a lot of bowl games in college; there's only one Super Bowl.

I could be called an expert on college bowl games since I was on Alabama teams that played in three of them. You didn't have all the photographers and the press conferences in college. The one thing that is similar is the feeling of playing in a big game. In college, I thought the bowl game was the biggest thing that every happened to me. But it doesn't compare with this.

Part of it is the money. But the other is knowing that when you play in the Super Bowl, and you win, you're the best in the world in your profession. It's also the difference between being a kid 22 years old and being a pro about 30 years old. Both games are fun but one is your job.

I'm not aware of who the writers are who are here. I don't pay much attention to writers. If Jim Murray of the Los Angeles *Times* walked in here right now, I wouldn't know who he is. The only ones I know, and am aware of, are some of the ones who cover our team all season long—Frank Cooney of the San Francisco *Examiner*, Tom LaMarre of the Oakland *Tribune*, and Dick O'Connor of the Palo Alto *Times*.

These are the guys who have been with us all year. From the first day of training camp. They don't have to ask dumb questions. They know all about us.

Every once in a while I'll recognize a writer from another city. I won't know his name but I can remember he's from Denver or Kansas City or other places we play every year. The guys who don't know me ask questions that people who do know me wouldn't ask. Those are the kind of questions I don't like to answer.

There are other guys who are trying to put you on the spot with questions. This one guy was trying to bait me into a verbal battle with Fran Tarkenton. I'm smart enough not to get involved in anything like that. He told me Fran said the Vikings were going to win and what did I think of that?

I told him the Raiders didn't come down here to lose. But he kept on trying to make me say something critical of Tarkenton or the Vikings.

Finally I got tired of that crap. I looked at him and said, "I don't know what you're trying to get me to say but whatever it is, I'm not going to do it."

I told him I wasn't going to get into a battle with Tarkenton so he finally went away.

In general, all the reporters have been good to me. They've been courteous and I've tried to be. I can understand their problem. There are all these different guys writing stories and each of them wants to have something different to write. The players have to realize that writers have a job to do just like we do. There's a time when we answer their questions at the press conferences. So they shouldn't bother us for interviews the rest of the time.

A lot depends on your mood. Sometimes when you've answered the same question 100 times, you really get mad the next time you hear it. But if you're in a good mood, you don't mind. You just give the same answer again and again and again. It can be tiresome and annoying but if you let it bother you, you won't be concentrating on playing football.

Like I said, there are not very many people who ask me a question I haven't heard before.

I'll talk football all day if I have the time. I really enjoy shooting the breeze about football. But I don't like to talk about my personal life. That belongs to me. If someone comes to me and asks for an interview, I'll do it if I can. But I'm not going to take my free time and give it all to other people.

It's tough to be down here in Newport Beach. Everyone knows we're at the Marriott Hotel. It gets so bad the players can't even go into the lobby. You can't fool around like we do at home or for road games during the regular season. There are always kids wanting autographs or someone wanting an interview.

You really don't have any time of your own unless you spend it in your room. That's what I do. I don't want any hassle. I don't like to tell kids I don't have time to sign autographs so I just don't go where they will ask me. The only time I had a chance to go out since we have been here was Thursday night. We had a short practice that day and a short meeting that night.

I went out to dinner with my family and some friends—my wife, my mother, and some people from back home in Alabama and some others from Newport Beach. We went to a restaurant across the street from the hotel—the Velvet Turtle. It's a nice place. We got one big table for all of us. There must have been about 15 at the table. It looked like the Last Supper. The table was so big it was hard to see the people at the other end.

We had a few rounds of drinks before dinner. I like some scotch now and then. I guess most quarterbacks drink scotch. Joe Namath does. Then I had scampi, the big shrimps in a garlic sauce. I really like seafood. When they brought the bill after dinner, I said I would split it with one of the other guys. It looked like the national debt. It was more than $200.

But this guy wouldn't let me pay—not even part of it. Then I got to thinking maybe he should pay the whole thing. He lives in Newport Beach. He's worth more money than he knows. He really doesn't know how much money he has. He's got a house on top of a hill overlooking the ocean. It cost about $350,000. He's got a yacht in his backyard and all that crap. He's really rich.

I didn't fight too hard to pay that bill. Doc, that's what we call this guy, is worth about $50 or $60 million. I figured he could handle it. So he finally paid it.

Fred Biletnikoff and his wife were there when we were. So was Pete Banaszak. Errol Mann was there with some of his friends. We sent drinks to each other's table. Freddie and Pete sent me a glass of chocolate milk with a cherry in it. I sent Errol Mann a glass of regular milk with a cherry in it.

We were just pulling each other's legs. It was really a good time. That was the only time we had a chance to relax all week and we enjoyed it.

I'm not going to do much else before the game. There's a big Fiesta Party in Pasadena Friday night and I got tickets for my family and friends. But none of the players are going. We have curfew. It takes two hours to drive to Pasadena and back and we wouldn't make curfew.

Coach Madden doesn't want any of the players to get involved in things like that. I'm happy just to kick back in my room and have a few whips . . . you know, a few drinks. Just relax and think about the game.

Then Saturday we'll go into Pasadena and work in

the Rose Bowl. That's no big thing for me, being in the Rose Bowl.

We'll have a meeting in the morning and then go out on the field and review everything, the offense and the defense and the special teams.

The Rose Bowl doesn't impress me. I mean, as a stadium. They're all about the same. The only stadium that did impress me was Yankee Stadium in New York where we played an exhibition game this season. That meant something to me because I was in the same stadium where Babe Ruth and Lou Gehrig and Mickey Mantle played.

And all the old football Giants played there too. That was special, just walking on the same field where great athletes had played. I want to tell people that I was in the same stadium where Babe Ruth played.

But there wasn't any feeling like that with the Rose Bowl. I went in there to see how the field was. I wanted to see if there was a crown on the field. I wanted to see the layout. That can affect how you throw the ball.

And I wanted to know where the clocks are. That's very important. It's a little thing but it's something you might forget in the excitement the day of the game.

I look to see what shape the field is in. I want to know if there are any slippery spots. And I want to know how much room there is in the back of the end zones.

I want to find out things I'll have to know when the game starts. Sometimes your depth perception is different on different fields. On a big wide-open field, the receiver looks a lot farther away than he really is.

A field where the stands are real close, the receiver looks like he's right on top of you.

The only way to find out is to go into a new stadium and look it over. These are little things but sometimes they can make the difference between winning and losing.

Other than that, the Rose Bowl is nothing special. I might be impressed with the size of it. What's it seat? 105,000. I guess it's the biggest stadium I will every play in. Everybody on the West Coast thinks the Rose Bowl is it. You know, the granddaddy of the bowl games. But I never watched it. I've always thought the bowl where the Southeastern Conference champion was playing was the big game. Of course, I'm prejudiced because I played at Alabama and they always went to bowl games. After I got out of college, the only bowl game I would watch was the one where the SEC champ was playing.

One thing about playing in the Rose Bowl: it could make me a unique football player. I wonder if there is anyone else who has been in four major bowl games. Of course, I'm substituting the pro Super Bowl for the Rose Bowl.

Playing in the Rose Bowl isn't anything special for some of our other players either. There are a lot of them who have played in it before. All the guys from USC–Clarence Davis, Mike Rae, Willie Hall, Manfred Moore, John Vella, Skip Thomas, and Charles Phillips–probably played here.

So did the guys from Ohio State–Jack Tatum, Morris Bradshaw, and Neal Colzie. Maybe Dave Dalby did too. He's from UCLA and they played in the Rose Bowl a couple of times. That should be good for our team, the experience of playing on this field.

Of course, Minnesota has some people who have

played in the Rose Bowl too. They have some guys from USC. I know Ron Yary played in the Rose Bowl.

Minnesota is an experienced team. They've played in the Super Bowl three times before. They haven't won but it's still good experience to even play in the game. The Vikings are a well-disciplined team. They're an older team and they are well coached. But I think we can beat them. They're good on defense. They don't do anything fancy. They just play straight up. They might make some changes but I don't think they'll do much.

They're just like us. They'll keep doing the things that got them to the Super Bowl. This isn't any time to be changing. The Vikings don't give you anything cheap. You have to work for everything you get when you play them. They seem to bend a little but they don't break.

We've seen films where the other team runs the ball very well against them. Then, when they get down close to scoring, Minnesota stops them. Those older guys they got on defense just seem to say, "Well, it's time to stop this team." And they do.

Teams just don't get in the end zone very often against the Vikings. If we expect to beat Minnesota, we have to keep the ball away from Fran Tarkenton. We have to maintain control on offense.

Tarkenton has lots of weapons. He's got three receivers who caught 50 or more passes during the regular season. And one of them, Chuck Foreman, also ran for more than 1,000 yards. That's why we have to control the ball so they don't get a chance to use all their weapons.

When we don't have the ball, we have to hope our defense can hold them or we get some turnovers. It seems like turnovers have always been a big factor in who wins the Super Bowl.

I haven't played that much against Minnesota. We played them only twice—both times in the 1973 season. They beat us both times—once in a preseason game and then again in the season opener.

I don't think that will make any difference, me not playing against them before. They haven't seen the Raiders with me playing quarterback either.

I just hope it's a wide-open game. I hate to go into a game and predetermine what we are going to do. I like to go in and do what's necessary to win. I want it to be a good game because the Super Bowl is always getting knocked for being conservative and dull. I'd like a game where there's a lot of passing, a lot of running, a lot of everything. I want the fans to get their $20 worth.

I want them to be able to say they saw the greatest Super Bowl ever played. And I want them to be able to say that because I had something to do with it.

Usually we run a very standard play on the first play of the game. It's Mark van Eeghen going up the middle. Maybe this time I'll throw a bomb to Cliff Branch on the very first play. If we miss on that, I'll come right back and throw another bomb.

I'd like a game like that. Maybe that's the way it will develop. But usually it doesn't. Teams come into the Super Bowl not wanting to make the big mistake that might put them in the hole or cost them the game.

I like games like our season opener with Pittsburgh, in which we scored three times in the last few minutes to win, 31–28. That's my kind of football. I think I threw 43 passes in that game. That's the way the Raiders play their best football. We win when we come out smokin'.

But sometimes you can't make yourself do that. It depends on the game situation. Maybe that's the wrong way to do it against the Vikings. Since they're older, there's always the possibility we could wear them down. Maybe we'll just keep hammering on them. Bam . . . bam . . . bam.

We've heard you can do that. That's what Los Angeles did but they didn't start soon enough. We may be able to just pound, pound, pound and make them break. There are several different ways to win. You have to be aware, during the game, of what's happening. That's when you decide what to do. There's no certain time. You just have to feel it. I can't say, "I've got to throw the ball on this play."

We have to just let it happen. If that means I throw the ball on every play, then that's what I'll do.

I think Fran Tarkenton likes to play that way too. He likes to spread the ball around on offense. He's really smart. Like I said, he's got three guys who caught 50 or more passes during the season. He uses them all. That puts a lot of pressure on the defense.

I noticed in the films of their playoff game with Los Angeles that Tarkenton didn't waste any time putting the ball in the air. He likes to play that way and so do I. I think he'll challenge our defense right away. And that's what I'm going to do to theirs.

I don't know that much about Tarkenton. I've never met him. Never even talked to him. I'll make a point of talking to him before the game. I try to talk to all the other quarterbacks I play against. While we're warming up, I might go over and shake hands with him. He's my counterpart and I want to know what he's like.

I have great respect for the other guys who do the same thing I do. I know what it takes to do it and I respect anyone else who does it.

I talk to Ken Anderson of Cincinnati whenever we play them. And I always talk to Terry Bradshaw of Pittsburgh if I have the chance. We're supposed to hate the Pittsburgh players but I like Terry. I always used to talk to Charlie Johnson when he played quarterback for Denver. He was a great guy—really smart.

When we played in New York this year, I talked to Joe Namath and Richard Todd, the Jet quarterbacks. That was really something. There were the three of us, all quarterbacks, and all from the University of Alabama.

But Tarkenton? I don't think I ever saw him play in college although he played at Georgia. I don't even remember his name. He's been playing so long, I probably wouldn't have been old enough to know who he was if I had seen him play in college.

The thing that amazes me about Tarkenton is his durability. I don't know how he has been able to run and scramble all these years and still stay together physically. He takes some good shots but he always lines up to play every Sunday. I admire any quarterback who can do that.

Every Sunday when Minnesota plays, he's there. He's not out with injuries and that's important to a team. They have to have that leader, someone they can count on being there every week. What is really amazing about Tarkenton is that he's run for more than 4,000 yards. Hell, there aren't very many people in the history of pro football who have gained that many yards.

And he's a quarterback.

It's got to be gratifying to him to be playing in the

Super Bowl. People used to knock him for not being a winner. But I think he's a winner. Just because he's played in the Super Bowl twice before and lost, doesn't make him a loser. How the hell many quarterbacks even get in the Super Bowl?

People used to knock him when he played for the Giants. They said a team couldn't win with a quarterback who was a scrambler. That's a lot of crap. Fran has proved that. He's a scrambler and he's playing in the Super Bowl again. There isn't a better passer in the history of football. He's passed for more yards than anyone else.

You just can't label him a loser.

I guess you could say there is a parallel between Tarkenton's career and mine. Oakland has been knocked for not winning the big games. and that means me. Our team has been frustrated by not even getting to the Super Bowl—that is, in my time.

Well, now we're here and so is Minnesota. I'm here and so is Fran Tarkenton.

This time we'll find out who the winner really is.

21

Afterthoughts

Pro football is tough. You have to learn to play with pain and pressure. If you're hurt, you might still have to play.

And the pressure? You never get away from that from the minute preseason practice starts until the final game.

First there's the pressure to make the team. Nobody can know what hell it is to go to preseason training camp and try to make the team unless he has been through it. It's too much for some players and they just walk away rather than take it.

After you make the team there's the pressure to do well. And if you do well, you have to win. You can't win most of the time. That isn't enough. You have to win the Super Bowl. Only then does the pressure go away and I didn't know what that felt like until we did it this year. It was like having a piano taken off my back.

I'm not saying the pressure bothers everyone. The good part of it is that the pressure only lasts six months of the year. It isn't like with some of the big executives who are under pressure all year round.

I like the pressure because I think it brings out the best in me. You earn your money when you play under the pressure to win the big games. And when you produce under pressure in the big games, like the Super Bowl, you earn the bucks. And that's what the whole damn game is all about.

I have pressure from Al Davis, our Managing General Partner, and I don't like that. No matter what you do, he thinks there's a better way to do it. He likes to project the image of the underworld type, a secretive type. He wears the dark glasses and the trench coat. He enjoys the image of being the street-smart kid who comes from the tough part of Brooklyn and makes good in pro football.

He does it by putting us in black uniforms and projecting the image of us as a mean, tough football team. I like that image too. He's not your average owner and the Raiders are not your average football team. And I guess you could say I'm not your average quarterback.

Our coach, John Madden, is not your average coach either. He lets us go and gives us a free wheel. He knows we've got a lot of loose guys and some renegades on our team. John handles the situation very well and I think he should get more credit than he does. I've grown to like Madden more and more each year.

I don't think we were that close early in my career because I wasn't playing and I can't be very friendly to the coach if I'm not the regular quarterback. Since I became the starter we've always gotten along very well. I respect his decisions and he's given me a free rein to call the plays. I enjoy watching him on the sidelines when I'm not playing. He stomps around like a big bear and he jumps up and down. He really puts on a show.

Once it comes to playing football, it's a different story. It's a brutal game and you either fish or cut bait. You can't take 260- and 270-pound men and tell them to tone it down.

They're out there to win because that's where the money is. You have to make the money when you're physically able and that isn't too long. You have to make it when you can or the team will get someone else who can do the job better.

There are a lot of fights and injuries in pro football. That's because of the competitive nature of the game. I don't see any problem about the brutality at this time because I think it's under control. Our game is prosperous and I hope it stays that way.

It seems like sometimes the only thing you read about in pro football are the fights and the injuries. It makes good reading, I guess. No one has lost his life in football because of brutality or fights. There have been broken noses and arms and knee injuries but no one is getting killed.

Hell, there's more brutality in the stands than there is on the field. We don't throw whiskey bottles at each other but the fans throw them at us. If they want to control something, they should do something about that. When we play in Pittsburgh, the fans come right down on the field after us. They shouldn't let the fans throw bottles, paper cups, snowballs, and pocket knives at us. That's the kind of stuff they should do something about. We're pretty big boys and can take care of ourselves but not when people are throwing bottles and knives at you.

Pep pills? I don't think players take pep pills or uppers to make themselves play better. They are taken, and I'm not going to say they aren't, because I think everyone knows that some players do take them. I don't know what it is that players take. I know I take pills for the pain in my knees. Lots of players take pills to ease the pain so they can play. That's part of the game—you have to learn to live with pain for six months of the year.

I've had two operations and my knees kill me during the season and I take something for that. But they are not pep pills. I think the pep pill thing is blown out of proportion. It isn't that big a deal.

A pro football player is going to have problems where there is an extra amount of money involved, where there is sex, booze, and all the attention that is paid to you because you're a pro athlete.

If you're not careful you start believing all that stuff. That isn't the way life is. The good things happen to a pro player when he's playing. After you've played that last game it stops happening. A lot of players make the mistake of thinking the good things are going to happen for the rest of their lives. It isn't, and that's where they get into trouble.

There are always women. There's a natural draw for women to athletes. We have a few bucks and a glamorous life and people always want to buy you drinks or buy you dinner.

There's a lot of publicity. We drive the big cars and wear the flashy clothes. Women like that sort of thing. You always run into them wherever you go, the groupies. There's never any trouble finding a woman if you want one because they are always around. You have women come up to you in a bar and first they want your autograph. The next thing you know they're laying all over you. You get phone calls and letters.

That kind of stuff taxes the hell out of a marriage. Sometimes your mind isn't where it should be, particularly when you're traveling.

Then, when you're home you might be watching TV and your wife thinks you're actually watching it. But you might be thinking about other things—not just football.

You don't pay as much attention to your wife as you should and she knows she's neglected. You're so involved with the pressure of football and the other things that you do ignore her.

Injuries can effect a marriage too. You're no fun to be around if you're always hurting. You're miserable all the time and that's no fun for anyone.

But all that stuff has to end. The balloon is going to burst and there won't be all that money anymore. Then those people who wanted to do things for you, and the women who would do things for you, won't be around anymore.

You have to realize that this thing right now is one big party . . . one big parade that isn't going to last forever.

You can play the game for 15 years and then you get out when you're 35. That isn't very much time and you still have your whole life ahead of you.

The way I look at it is that it will be a merry-go-round for me for another five or six years. I'm going to try and win as many damn games as I can but I'm not going to take myself too seriously.

This thing is going to end and then I'm going to settle down to a normal life and raise children.

Basically, that's the way I feel about what I do for a living. I wish I could do it forever. I wish I could do it until I'm 100 years old. I would like to lead the league in passing for 99 years and be second the other year.

But you can't play forever. You have to make the most of it while you can.

Appendix

Ken Stabler's Alabama Record

SOPHOMORE (1965)	RUSHING					PASSING						TOTAL	
Game	No.	Gain	Loss	Net	TD	Att.	Comp.	Pct.	I	Yds.	TD	Plays	Yds.
Georgia	—	—	—	—	—	—	—	—	—	—	—	—	—
Tulane	6	33	0	33	0	6	1	14.4	0	6	0	12	39
Ole Miss	—	—	—	—	—	—	—	—	—	—	—	—	—
Vanderbilt ...	2	4	0	4	0	0	0	00.0	0	0	0	2	4
Tennessee ...	19	85	3	82	0	1	0	00.0	0	0	0	20	82
Fla. State	8	62	0	62	0	1	0	00.0	0	0	0	9	62
Miss. State ..	—	—	—	—	—	—	—	—	—	—	—	—	—
L. S. U.	10	42	0	42	0	1	0	00.0	0	0	0	11	42
S. Carolina ..	8	84	0	84	1	0	0	00.0	0	0	0	8	84
Auburn	8	21	0	21	0	2	2	100.0	0	20	0	10	41
Totals	**61**	**331**	**3**	**328**	**1**	**11**	**3**	**27.3**	**0**	**26**	**0**	**72**	**354**
Orange Bowl .	—	—	—	—	—	—	—	—	—	—	—	—	—

JUNIOR (1966)	RUSHING					PASSING						TOTAL	
Game	No.	Gain	Loss	Net	TD	Att.	Comp.	Pct.	I	Yds.	TD	Plays	Yds.
La. Tech	7	33	0	33	1	5	2	40.0	0	111	2	12	144
Ole Miss	15	33	13	20	0	19	16	84.2	0	144	1	34	164
Clemson	9	39	0	39	1	8	7	87.5	0	93	2	17	132

JUNIOR (1966)	RUSHING					PASSING						TOTAL	
Game	No.	Gain	Loss	Net	TD	Att.	Comp.	Pct.	I	Yds.	TD	Plays	Yds.
Tennessee ...	18	59	3	56	1	15	7	46.7	0	72	0	33	128
Vanderbilt ...	10	61	0	61	0	6	3	50.0	1	27	0	16	88
Miss. State ..	9	74	10	64	0	9	3	33.3	2	23	0	18	87
L. S. U.	8	28	11	17	0	6	5	83.3	0	93	0	14	110
S. Carolina ..	3	21	0	21	0	9	7	77.8	1	66	0	12	87
Sou. Miss ...	5	35	1	34	0	21	13	61.9	1	158	3	26	192
Auburn	9	52	1	51	0	16	11	68.8	0	169	1	25	220
Season Totals	**93**	**435**	**39**	**397**	**3**	**114**	**74**	**64.9**	**5**	**956**	**9**	**207**	**1353**
Sugar Bowl ..	10	58	18	40	1	17	12	70.6	0	218	1	27	258

SENIOR (1967)	RUSHING					PASSING						TOTAL	
Game	No.	Gain	Loss	Net	TD	Att.	Comp.	Pct.	I	Yds.	TD	Plays	Yds.
Fla. State ...	11	23	25	- 2	1	20	11	55.0	2	192	2	31	190
Sou. Miss ...	7	19	29	-10	0	26	19	73.1	0	191	3	33	181
Ole Miss	9	32	23	9	1	21	12	57.1	1	119	1	30	128
Vanderbilt ...	12	32	15	17	1	11	6	54.5	0	119	2	23	136
Tennessee ...	18	65	40	25	1	32	15	46.9	5	154	0	50	179
Clemson	12	15	50	-35	0	15	9	60.0	0	135	0	27	100
Miss. State ..	6	12	11	1	0	17	11	64.7	2	96	0	23	97
L. S. U.	13	43	21	22	0	16	9	56.3	1	83	0	29	105
S. Carolina ..	9	35	24	11	0	15	8	53.3	1	113	1	24	124
Auburn	14	88	13	75	1	5	3	60.0	1	12	0	19	87
Season Totals	**111**	**394**	**251**	**103**	**5**	**178**	**103**	**57.9**	**13**	**1214**	**9**	**289**	**1327**
Cotton Bowl .	12	22	21	1	2	26	16	61.5	3	179	0	28	180
Career	**275**	**1188**	**311**	**831**	**10**	**320**	**192**	**60.0**	**18**	**2414**	**19**	**595**	**3292**

Ken Stabler's Oakland Record

PASSING

Year	Att.	Comp.	Pct.	Yds.	TD	Int.	LP
1970	7	2	28.6	52	0	1	33
1971	48	24	50.0	268	1	4	23
1972	74	44	59.5	524	4	3	22
1973	260	163	62.7	1997	14	10	80
1974	310	178	57.4	2469	26	12	67
1975	293	171	58.4	2296	16	24	53
1976	291	194	66.7	2737	27	17	88
Totals	**1283**	**776**	**60.4**	**10,343**	**88**	**71**	**—**

RUSHING

Year	No.	Yds.	Avg.	TD	LR
1970	1	—4	—4.0	0	—4
1971	4	29	7.3	2	18
1972	6	27	4.5	0	15
1973	21	101	4.8	0	13
1974	12	—2	—1.6	1	6
1975	6	—5	—0.8	0	0
1976	7	—2	—0.3	1	5
Totals	**57**	**144**	**2.5**	**4**	**—**

SCORING

Year	TD	PAT	FG	Total
1971	2	0	0	12
1974	1	0	0	6
1976	1	0	0	6
Totals	**4**	**0**	**0**	**24**

SUPER BOWL

Year	Att.	Comp.	Pct.	Yds.	TD	Int.	LP
1976	19	12	63.1	180	1	0	48

Super Bowl XI Statistics

	Raiders (32)	Vikings (14)
First downs	21	20
Rushes-yards	52—266	26—71
Passing yards	163	282
Return yards	134	14
Passes	12—19—0	24—44—2
Punts	5—32	7—38
Fumbles-lost	0—0	1—1
Penalties-yards	4—30	2—25

Oakland	**0**	**16**	**3**	**13—32**
Minnesota	**0**	**0**	**7**	**7—14**

Oak—FG Mann 24
Oak—Casper 1 pass from Stabler (Mann kick)
Oak—Banaszak 1 run (kick failed)
Oak—FG Mann 40
Min—S. White 8 pass from Tarkenton (Cox kick)
Oak—Banaszak 2 run (Mann kick)
Oak—Brown 75 interception return (kick failed)
Min—Voigt 13 pass from Lee (Cox kick)

INDIVIDUAL LEADERS

RUSHING—Oakland, Davis 16-137, van Eeghen 18-73, Garrett 4-19, Banaszak 10-19, Ginn 2-9, Rae 2-9. Minnesota, Foreman 17-44, McClanahan 3-8, Miller 2-4, Lee 1-4, S. White 1-7, S. Johnson 2-9.

RECEIVING—Oakland, Casper 4-70, Biletnikoff 4-79, Branch 3-20, Garrett 1-11. Minnesota, Foreman 5-62, Rashad 3-53, Miller 4-19, Voigt 4-49, S. White 5-77, S. Johnson 3-26.

PASSING—Oakland, Stabler 12-19-0, 180 yards; Rae 0-0-0, 0. Minnesota, Tarkenton 17-35-2, 205; Lee 7-9-0, 81.

INTERCEPTIONS—Oakland, W. Hall 1-16; Brown 1-75.

PUNTING—Oakland, Guy 4-162, avg. 40.5 (fifth punt blocked), Minnesota, Clabo, 7-265, avg. 37.9.

PUNT RETURNS—Oakland, Colzie 4-43. Minnesota, Willis 3-14.

KICKOFF RETURNS—Oakland, Garrett 2-47, Siani 1-0. Minnesota, Willis 3-57, S. White 4-79.

A—100,421: actual turnstile count. Sellout of 103,424 was announced.

Oakland's 1976 Record

September 12—Oakland 31, Pittsburgh 28
September 20—Oakland 24, Kansas City 21
September 26—Oakland 14, Houston 13
October 3—New England 48, Oakland 17
October 10—Oakland 27, San Diego 17
October 17—Oakland 17, Denver 10
October 24—Oakland 18, Green Bay 14
October 31—Oakland 19, Denver 6
November 7—Oakland 28, Chicago 27
November 14—Oakland 21, Kansas City 10
November 21—Oakland 26, Philadelphia 7
November 28—Oakland 49, Tampa Bay 16
December 6—Oakland 35, Cincinnati 20
December 12—Oakland 24, San Diego 0

Playoffs
December 18—Oakland 24, New England 21
December 26—Oakland 24, Pittsburgh 7

Super Bowl
January 9—Oakland 32, Minnesota 14

Oakland Raiders' All-Time Roster

AGAJANIAN, Ben	New Mexico	K	1962
ALLEN, Dalva	Houston	DE	1962-63-64
ALLEN, Jackie	Baylor	DB	1969
ARCHER, Dan	Oregon	T	1967
ARMSTRONG, Ramon	TCU	T	1960
ASAD, Doug	Northwestern	TE	1960-61
ATKINS, Pervis	New Mex. State	WR	1965-66
ATKINSON, George	Morris Brown	DB	1968-76
BANASZAK, Pete	Miami (Fla.)	RB	1966-76
BANKS, Estes	Colorado	RB	1967
BANKSTON, Warren	Tulane	TE	1973-76
BANSAVAGE, Al	Southern Calif.	LB	1961
BARBEE, Joe	Kent State	T	1960
BARNES, Larry	Colorado A&M	LB	1960
BARNES, Rodrigo	Rice	LB	1976
BARRETT, Jan	Fresno State	TE	1963-64
BENSON, Duane	Hamline	LB	1967-71
BILETNIKOFF, Fred	Florida State	WR	1965-76
BIRD, Rodger	Kentucky	DB	1967-71
BIRDWELL, Dan	Houston	DT	1962-69
BISHOP, Sonny	Fresno State	G	1963
BLANDA, George	Kentucky	QB-K	1967-75
BONNESS, Rick	Nebraska	LB	1976
BOYDSTON, Max	Oklahoma	TE	1962
BOYNTON, George	East Texas State	DB	1962
BRADSHAW, Morris	Ohio State	WR	1974-76
BRANCH, Cliff	Colorado	WR	1972-76
BRAVO, Alex	California Poly	DB	1960-61
BREWINGTON, Jim	No. Carolina Col	T	1961
BROWN, Bob	Nebraska	T	1971-73
BROWN, Charles	Houston	T	1962
BROWN, Doug	Fresno State	DT	1964
BROWN, Willie	Grambling	DB	1967-76
BUDNESS, Bill	Boston Univ.	LB	1964-70
BUEHLER, George	Stanford	G	1969-76
BUIE, Drew	Catawba	WR	1969-71
BURCH, Gerald	Georgia Tech	TE	1961
CAMPBELL, Stan	Iowa State	G	1962
CANNAVINO, Joe	Ohio State	DB	1960-61
CANNON, Billy	LSU	TE	1964-69
CARROLL, Joe	Pittsburgh	LB	1972-73
CARTER, Louis	Maryland	RB	1975
CASPER, Dave	Notre Dame	TE	1974-76
CAVALLI, Carmen	Richmond	DE	1960
CHESTER, Raymond	Morgan State	TE	1970-72
CHURCHWELL, Hansen	Mississippi	DT	1960

CLINE, Tony	Miami (Fla.)	DE	1970-75
COLZIE, Neal	Ohio State	DB	1975-76
CONNERS, Dan	Miami (Fla.)	LB	1964-74
COOLBAUGH, Bob	Richmond	WR	1961
COSTA, Dave	Utah	DT	1963-65
CRAIG, Dobie	Howard Payne	WR	1962-63
CROW, Wayne	California	RB-DB	1960-61
DALBY, Dave	UCLA	C-G	1972-76
DANIELS, Clemon	Prairie View	RB	1961-67
DANIELS, David	Florida A&M	DT	1966
DAVIDSON, Ben	Washington	DE	1964-71
DAVIDSON, Cotton	Baylor	QB	1962-69
DAVIS, Clarence	Southern Calif.	RB	1971-76
DENNERY, Mike	So. Mississippi	LB	1974-75
DePOYSTER, Jerry	Wyoming	K	1971-72
DESKINS, Don	Michigan	G	1960
DICKEY, Eldridge	Tennessee State	WR	1968-71
DICKINSON, Bo	So. Mississippi	RB	1964
DIEHL, John	Virginia	DT	1965
DITTRICH, John	Wisconsin	G	1960
DIXON, Hewritt	Florida A&M	RB	1966-68-69-70
DORSEY, Dick	Southern Calif.	OE	1962
DOTSON, Al	Grambling	DT	1968-70
DOUGHERTY, Bob	Kentucky	LB	1960-63
EASON, John	Florida A&M	TE	1968
EDWARDS, Lloyd	San Diego State	TE	1969
EISCHEID, Mike	Upper Iowa	K	1966-71
ELLISON, Glenn	Arkansas	RB	1971
ENIS, Hunter	TCU	QB	1962
ENYART, Bill	Oregon State	LB	1971
FAIRBAND, Bill	Colorado	LB	1967-68
FICCA, Dan	Southern Calif.	G	1962
FIELDS, George	Bakersfield J.C.	DT	1960-61
FINNERAN, Garry	Southern Calif.	DT	1961
FLEMING, George	Washington	RB	1961
FLORES, Tom	Pacific	QB	1960-61,63-66
FULLER, Charles	S.F. State	RB	1961-62
GALLEGOS, Chon	San Jose State	QB	1962
GARNER, Bob	Fresno State	DB	1961-62
GARRETT, Carl	N. Mex. Highlands	RB	1976
GIBSON, Claude	No. Carolina St.	DB	1963-65
GILLETT, Fred	L.A. State	OE	1964
GINN, Hubert	Florida A&M	RB	1976
GIPSON, Tom	North Texas State	DT	1971
GOLDSTEIN, Alan	North Carolina	WR	1960
GRAYSON, David	Oregon	DB	1965-70
GREEN, Charley	Wittenberg	QB	1966
GUY, Louie	Mississippi	DB	1964

GUY, Ray	So. Mississippi	K	1973-76
HAGBERG, Roger	Minnesota	FB	1965-69
HALL, Willie	USC	LB	1976
HARDY, Charles	San Jose State	WR	1960-62
HARRIS, John	Santa Monica	DB	1960-61
HART, Harold	Texas Southern	RB	1974-75
HARVEY, James	Mississippi	G	1966-71
HAWKINS, Wayne	Pacific	G	1960-70
HEINRICH, Don	Washington	QB	1962
HENDRICKS, Ted	Miami	LB	1975-76
HERMANN, Dick	Florida State	LB	1965
HEROCK, Ken	West Virginia	TE	1963-65,67
HIGHSMITH, Don	Michigan State	RB	1970-72
HOISINGTON, Al	Pasadena Col.	WR	1960
HOPKINS, Jerry	Texas A&M	LB	1968
HUBBARD, Marv	Colgate	RB	1969-75
HUDSON, Bob	NE Oklahoma	RB	1973-74
HUMM, David	Nebraska	QB	1975-76
IRONS, Gerald	Maryland (ES)	LB	1970-75
JACKSON, Bobby	New Mex. State	RB	1964
JACKSON, Richard	Southern	LB	1966
JACOBS, Proverb	California	T	1963-64
JAGIELSKI, Harry	Indiana	DT	1961
JAKOWENKO, George	Syracuse	K	1974
JELACIC, Jon	Minnesota	DE	1961-64
JENNINGS, Rich	Maryland	RB-WR	1976
JOHNSON, Monte	Nebraska	LB	1973-76
JONES, Horace	Louisville	DE	1971-75
JONES, Jim	Washington	LB	1961
JOYNER, L.C.	Diablo Valley	DB	1960
KEATING, Tom	Michigan	DT	1966-72
KENT, Greg	Utah	T	1966
KEYES, Bob	San Diego Univ.	B	1960
KLEIN, Dick	Iowa	T	1963-64
KOCOUREK, Dave	Wisconsin	TE	1967-68
KOEGEL, Warren	Penn State	C	1971
KORVER, Kelvin	Northwestern (IA)	DT	1973-75
KOWALCZYK, Walt	Michigan State	RB	1961
KOY, TED	Texas	TE	1970
KRAKOSKI, Joe	Illinois	DB	1963-66
KRUSE, Bob	Wayne State	G	1967-68
KWALICK, Ted	Penn State	TE	1975
LAMONICA, Daryle	Notre Dame	QB	1967-74
LARSCHIED, Jack	Pacific	OB	1960-61
LARSON, Paul	California	QB	1960
LASKEY, Bill	Michigan	LB	1966-70
LASSITER, Isaac	St. Augustine	DE	1965-69
LAWRENCE, Henry	Florida A&M	T	1974-76

LAWRENCE, Larry	Iowa	QB	1974-75
LEWIS, Harold	Houston	RB	1962
LOCKLIN, Billy Ray	New Mex. State	G	1960
LOTT, Billy	Mississippi	OB	1960
LOUDERBACK, Tom	San Jose State	LB	1960-61
MACON, Ed	Pacific	DB	1960
MacKINNON, Jacque	Colgate	TE	1970
MANN, Errol	North Dakota	K	1976
MANOUKIAN, Don	Stanford	G	1960
MARINOVICH, Marv	Southern Calif.	G	1965
MATSOS, Arch	Michigan State	LB	1963-65
MATUSZAK, John	Tampa	DT	1976
MAXWELL, Tom	Texas A&M	DB	1971-73
MAYBERRY, Doug	Utah State	RB	1963
McCLOUGHAN, Kent	Nebraska	DB	1965-70
McFARLAN, Nyle	Brigham Young	DB	1960
McMATH, Herb	Morningside	DE	1976
McMillin, Jim	Colorado State	DB	1963-64
McMURTRY, Chuck	Whittier	DT	1962-63
MEDLIN, Dan	No. Carolina State	G	1974-76
MENDENHALL, Terry	San Diego State	LB	1971-72
MERCER, Mike	Arizona State	K	1963-65
MILLER, Alan	Boston College	FB	1961,63-65
MILLER, Bill	Miami	WR	1964,66-68
MINGO, Gene	None	K	1964-65
MIRICH, Rex	Arizona State	DT	1964-66
MISCHAK, Bob	West Point	G	1963-65
MITCHELL, Tom	Bucknell	TE	1966
MIX, Ron	Southern Calif.	T	1971
MONTALBO, Mel	Utah State	DB	1962
MOORE, Bob	Stanford	TE	1971-75
MOORE, Manfred	USC	RB	1976
MORRIS, Riley	Florida A&M	DE	1960-62
MORRISON, Dave	S.W. Texas State	DB	1968
MORROW, Tom	So. Mississippi	DB	1962-64
MOSTARDI, Rich	Kent State	DB	1962
MURDOCK, Jesse	Calif. Western	RB	1963
NICKLAS, Pete	Baylor	T	1962
NORRIS, Jim	Houston	DT	1962-63
NOVSEK, Joe	Tulsa	DE	1962
OATS, Carleton	Florida A&M	DT	1965-72
OGAS, Dave	San Diego State	LB	1968
OGLESBY, Paul	USLA	T	1960
OLIVER, Ralph	Southern Calif.	LB	1968-69
OSBORNE, Clancy	Arizona State	LB	1963-64
OTTO, Gus	Missouri	LB	1965-72
OTTO, Jim	Miami (Fla.)	C	1960-74
PAPAC, Nick	Fresno State	QB	1961

PARILLI, Babe	Kentucky	QB	1960
PETERS, Volney	Southern Calif.	DT	1961
PHILLIPS, Charles	Southern Calif.	DB	1975-76
PHILLIPS, Jess	Michigan State	RB	1975
PHILYAW, Charles	Texas Southern	DE	1976
PITTS, Frank	Southern	WR	1974
POWELL, Art	San Jose State	WR	1963-66
POWELL, Charlie	None	DE	1960-61
POWERS, Warren	Nebraska	DB	1963-68
PREBOLA, Gene	Boston Univ.	TE	1960
PROUT, Bob	Knox	DB	1974
PYLE, Palmer	Michigan State	G	1966
QUEEN, Jeff	Morgan State	RB-TE	1973
RAE, Mike	USC	QB	1976
REYNOLDS, Billy	Pittsburgh	OB	1960
REYNOLDS, M.C.	LSU	QB	1961
RICE, Floyd	Alcorn A&M	DE	1976
RICE, Harold	Tennessee State	DE	1971
RICE, Ken	Auburn	T	1964-65
RIDLEHUBER, Preston	Georgia	RB	1968
RIEVES, Charles	Houston	LB	1962-63
RIVERA, Hank	Oregon State	DB	1962
ROBERSON, Bo	Cornell	WR	1962-65
ROBERTS, Cliff	Illinois	DT	1961
RODERICK, John	SMU	WR	1968
ROEDEL, Herb	Marquette	G	1961
ROWE, Dave	Penn State	DT	1975-76
RUBKE, Karl	Southern Calif.	DE	1968
SABAL, Ron	Purdue	T	1960-61
SCHMAUTZ, Ray	San Diego State	LB	1966
SCHUH, Harry	Memphis State	T	1965-70
SEILER, Paul	Notre Dame	T	1971-73
SHAW, Glenn	Kentucky	RB	1963-64
SHELL, Arthur	Maryland (ES)	T	1968-76
SHERMAN, Rod	Southern Calif.	WR	1967,69-71
SHIRKEY, George	S.F. Austin	DT	1962
SIANI, Mike	Villanova	WR	1972-76
SIMPSON, Jack	Mississippi	LB	1962-64
SIMPSON, Willie	S.F. State	RB	1962
SISTRUNK, Otis	No College	DT	1972-76
SLIGH, Richard	N. Carolina Coll.	T	1967
SLOUGH, Greg	Southern Calif.	LB	1971-72
SMITH, Bubba	Michigan State	DE	1973-74
SMITH, Charles	Utah	RB	1968-74
SMITH, Hal	UCLA	DT	1961
SMITH, James	Compton	RB	1960
SMITH, Ron	Wisconsin	DB	1974
SMITH, Willie	Michigan	RB	1961
SOMMER, Mike	Geo. Washington	RB	1963

SPENCER, Ollie	Kansas	G	1963
STABLER, Ken	Alabama	QB	1970-76
STONE, Jack	Oregon	T	1961-62
STREIGEL, Bill	Pacific	LB	1960
SVIHUS, Bob	Southern Calif.	T	1965-70
SWEENEY, Steve	California	WR	1973
SYLVESTER, Steve	Notre Dame	C-G	1975-76
TATUM, Jack	Ohio State	DB	1971-76
TERESA, Tony	San Jose State	RB	1960
THOMAS, Alonzo	Southern Calif.	DB	1972-75
THOMS, Art	Syracuse	DT	1969-76
TODD, Larry	Arizona State	RB	1965-70
TRASK, Orville	Rice	DT	1962
TRUAX, Dalton	Tulane	DT	1960
TYSON, Richard	Tulsa	G	1966
UPSHAW, Eugene	Texas A&I	G	1967-76
URENDA, Herman	Pacific	OE	1963
VALDEZ, Vernon	San Diego Univ.	DB	1962
van EEGHEN, Mark	Colgate	RB	1974-76
VELLA, John	Southern Calif.	G-T	1972-76
VILLAPIANO, Phil	Bowling Green	LB	1971-76
VOIGHT, Bob	L.A. State	DE	1961
WARREN, Jimmy	Illinois	DB	1970-74
WARZEKA, Ron	Montana State	DE	1960
WEATHERS, Carl	San Diego State	LB	1970-71
WEAVER, Gary	Fresno State	LB	1973
WELLS, Warren	Texas Southern	WR	1967-70
WHITE, Eugene	Florida A&M	RB	1962
WILLIAMS, Howie	Howard	DB	1964-69
WILLIAMS, Willie	Grambling	DB	1966
WILLIAMSON, Fred	Northwestern	DB	1961-64
WILLIAMSON, J.R.	Louisiana Tech	LB	1964-67
WILSON, Nemiah	Grambling	DB	1968-74
WINANS, Jeff	USC	DT	1976
WOOD, Dick	Auburn	QB	1965
WYATT, Alvin	Bethune-Cookman	DB	1970
YOUSO, Frank	Minnesota	T	1963-65
ZECHER, Rich	Utah State	T	1965